ARGUING ABOUT WAR

Michael Walzer

ARGUING about WAR

Yale University Press • *New Haven & London*

Published with assistance from the Kingsley Trust
Association Publication Fund established by the
Scroll and Key Society of Yale College.

Designed by Nancy Ovedovitz and set in Janson Oldstyle
type by Keystone Typesetting, Inc. Printed in the United
States of America by R. R. Donnelley, Harrisonburg,
Virginia

Library of Congress Cataloging-in-Publication Data
Walzer, Michael.
Arguing about war / Michael Walzer.
p. cm.
Includes bibliographical references and index.
ISBN 0-300-10365-4
1. War. 2. Just war doctrine. 3. Intervention (International
law). 4. World politics — 1989–. I. Title.
U21.2.W34497 2004
172'.42 — dc22   2003067409

A catalogue record for this book is available from the
British Library.

The paper in this book meets the guidelines for
permanence and durability of the Committee on
Production Guidelines for Book Longevity of the Council
on Library Resources.

2 4 6 8 10 9 7 5 3 1

For JBW, always

CONTENTS

CONTENTS

INTRODUCTION

Clausewitz's famous line, that war is the continuation of politics by other means, was probably meant to be provocative, but it seems to me obviously true. And the claim is equally obvious the other way around: politics is the continuation of war by other means. It is very important, however, that the means are different. Politics is a form of peaceful contention, and war is organized violence. All the participants, all the activists and militants, survive a political defeat (unless the victor is a tyrant, at war with his own people), whereas many participants, soldiers and civilians alike, do not survive a military defeat — or a victory either. War kills, and that is why the argument about war is so intense.

The theory of just war, which I defended in *Just and Unjust Wars* (1977) and which is further developed and applied in the essays collected here, is, first of all, an argument about the moral standing of warfare as a human activity. The argument is twofold: that war is sometimes justifiable and that the conduct of war is always subject to moral criticism. The first of these propositions is denied by pacifists, who believe that war is a criminal act; and the second is denied by realists, for whom "all's fair in love and war": *inter arma silent leges* (in time of war, the laws are silent). So just war theorists set themselves in opposition to pacifists and realists, of whom there are a great number, although some of the pacifists are selective in their opposition to war and some of the realists have been heard, in the heat of battle, to express moral sentiments.

But just war theory is not only an argument about war in

general; it is also the ordinary language in which we argue about particular wars. It is the way most of us talk when we join political debates about whether to fight and how to fight. Ideas like self-defense and aggression, war as a combat between combatants, the immunity of noncombatants, the doctrine of proportionality, the rules of surrender, the rights of prisoners — these are our common heritage, the product of many centuries of arguing about war. "Just war" is nothing more than a theoretical version of all this, designed to help us resolve, or at least to think clearly about, the problems of definition and application.

I want to address two criticisms of just war theory, because I have heard them often — specifically in response to some of the pieces collected here. The first is that those of us who defend and apply the theory are moralizing war, and by doing that we are making it easier to fight. We take away the stigma that should always be attached to the business of killing, which is what war always and necessarily is. When we define the criteria by which war and the conduct of war can be judged, we open the way for favorable judgments. Many of these judgments will be ideological, partisan, or hypocritical in character and, therefore, subject to criticism, but some of them, given the theory, will be right: some wars and some acts of war will turn out to be "just." How can that be, when war is so terrible?

But *just* is a term of art here; it means justifiable, defensible, even morally necessary (given the alternatives) — and that is all it means. All of us who argue about the rights and wrongs of war agree that justice in the strong sense, the sense that it has in domestic society and everyday life, is lost as soon as the fighting begins. War is a zone of radical coercion, in which justice is always under a cloud. Still, sometimes we are right to enter the zone. As someone who grew up during World War II, this seems to me another obvious point. There are acts of aggression and acts of cruelty that we ought to resist, by force if necessary. I would have thought that our experience with Nazism ended this particular argument, but the argument goes one — hence the disagreements about humanitarian intervention that I address in a number of these essays. The use of military force to stop the killing in Rwanda would have been, in my view, a just war. And if that judgment "moralizes" military force and makes it easier to use — well, I wish it had been easier to use in Africa in 1994.

The second criticism of just war theory is that it frames wars in the wrong way. It focuses our attention on the immediate issues at stake before the war begins — in the case of the recent Iraq war, for example, on inspections, disarmament, hidden weapons, and so on — and then on the conduct of the war, battle by battle; and so it avoids larger questions about imperial ambition and the global struggle for resources and power. It is as if citizens of the ancient world had focused narrowly on the conflict between Rome and some other city-state over whether a treaty had been violated, as the Romans always claimed in the lead-up to their attack, and never discussed the long history of Roman expansion. But if critics can distinguish between concocted excuses for war and actual reasons, why can't the rest of us do the same thing? Just war theory has no fixed temporal limits; it can be used to analyze a long chain of events as readily as a short one. Indeed, how can imperial warfare be criticized if not in just war terms? What other language, what other theory, is available for such a critique? Aggressive wars, wars of conquest, wars to extend spheres of influence and establish satellite states, wars for economic aggrandizement — all these are unjust wars.

Just war is a theory made for criticism. But that doesn't mean that every war has to be criticized. When I defended the recent war in Afghanistan, some of my own critics claimed that since I had opposed the American war in Vietnam and many of our little wars and proxy wars in Central America, I was now being inconsistent. But that is like saying that a doctor who diagnoses one patient with cancer is then obliged to provide a similar diagnosis for every other patient. The same medical criteria yield different diagnoses in different cases. And the same moral criteria yield different judgments in different wars. Still, the judgments are controversial, even when we agree on criteria: read my piece on Kosovo, and then look for a second opinion. You won't have any difficulty finding one that differs from my own; and that is true for all my other arguments, too. The fact that we disagree, however, doesn't make just war different from any other moral (or political) concept. We give different accounts of the same military action, and we also give different accounts of the same election. We disagree about corruption, discrimination, and inequality even when we talk about all three in the common language of democratic theory. Disagreements don't invalidate a theory; the theory, if it is a good one, makes the disagreements more coherent and comprehensible.

Ongoing disagreements, together with the rapid pace of political change, sometimes require revisions of a theory. My own judgments since *Just and Unjust Wars* have been, I like to think, fairly consistent. But I have changed my mind or shifted the emphasis of my arguments about a few things, which it seems right to acknowledge here. Faced with the sheer number of recent horrors — with massacre and ethnic cleansing in Bosnia and Kosovo; in Rwanda, the Sudan, Sierra Leone, the Congo, and

Liberia; in East Timor (and earlier, in Cambodia and Bangladesh) — I have slowly become more willing to call for military intervention. I haven't dropped the presumption against intervention that I defended in my book, but I have found it easier and easier to override the presumption. And faced with the reiterated experience of state failure, the reemergence of a form of politics that European historians call "bastard feudalism," dominated by warring gangs and would-be charismatic leaders, I have become more willing to defend long-term military occupations, in the form of protectorates and trusteeships, and to think of nation-building as a necessary part of postwar politics. Both of these shifts also require me to recognize the need for an expansion of just war theory. *Jus ad bellum* (which deals with the decision to go to war) and *jus in bello* (which deals with the conduct of the battles) are its standard elements, first worked out by Catholic philosophers and jurists in the Middle Ages. Now we have to add to those two an account of *jus post bellum* (justice after the war). I wrote a section on justice in settlements in *Just and Unjust Wars*, but it is much too brief and doesn't even begin to address many of the problems that have arisen in places like Kosovo and East Timor and, recently, in Iraq. More work is necessary here, in both the theory and practice of peacemaking, military occupation, and political reconstruction.

I have called these arguments about war "ongoing." In fact, they are probably endless. There has been an effort to abolish war — it is reflected in the U.N. charter — by treating aggression as a criminal act and describing any response as a "police action." This is what the Chinese call, or used to call, "rectification of names." But we can't change reality by changing the way we talk about it, as we can see in the original case: the U.N. police action in Korea in 1950 is called a war by all its historians. Still, the impulse lingers. We saw it at work in the immediate aftermath of September 11, 2001, when many people in the United States and Europe insisted that the attack was a crime and that we should not go to war (as we soon did in Afghanistan) but should call the police instead. I thought of this as the "dial 911" response to 9/11, and it would have been a perfectly plausible response if anyone were answering the phone. In a global state with a monopoly on the legitimate use of force, calling the police would be the right response to violence. Crime, the pursuit of the criminal by the police, and the trial and punishment of the criminal — these three would exhaust the field of action; we would read about war only in the history books. But that is not a description of the world we live in, and even if a global state ought to be our goal (I raise some doubts about that in the last of these essays), it is a great mistake to pretend that we are already there.

So we are doomed to continue arguing about war; it is a necessary activity of democratic citizens. Just war theory has had an academic history in recent years, but that is not the history that is represented here. None of these essays was published in a standard academic journal. Almost all of them were written for political magazines, or they were lectures to citizens and soldiers (two of them at military academies, a couple more at university teach-ins). They are all political acts, and that is my excuse for the occasional reiterations of the same argument; I have cut some of these but not all. Political theorists aim at originality, but politics is an art of repetition. "Try, try again" is a maxim not only for activists but also for publicists: if an argument doesn't convince enough people the first time you make it, there is nothing to do but make it again.

The first group of essays deals with general issues like nuclear deterrence, terrorism, and humanitarian intervention. They are in part attempts at theoretical clarification, but they are also, and more importantly, political engagements. When I wrote them, I was joining debates in progress. I suppose that I was joining the debates as a theorist, but my interest was political, not philosophical. This is even more true of the second group of essays, all of which were written in response to particular wars. They were published before, during, and after the fighting, but always as part of a public debate about a particular time and place and a particular set of political or military policies. The last essay is my effort to imagine a future in which war might play a less significant part in our lives. It's not a utopian account of international society, only a description of a less-bad arrangement than we have now. In fact, that is the aim of most of the arguments made by just war theorists; we may be opposed to "realism" but we are not unrealistic, as I hope these essays demonstrate. The point of seeking justice even under the cloud of war is to avoid disasters. When we aim at more than that, as we should, we will need the guidance of different political theories.

In addition to cutting (some) repetitions, I have also added, always in brackets, a few references to earlier or later articles in this collection. When a particular piece was published in different versions in U.S. and European magazines, or when it was published first in a magazine and later in a book, I have felt free to choose the version that reads best today. I have cut a few parenthetical remarks, as well as a few local and immediate references, now outdated. A number of the articles have endnotes, and others don't; I haven't attempted to provide a uniform system of citation. In a few places I have restored a word or phrase cut or changed by an editor. Otherwise, I have made no revisions; I leave the benefits of hindsight to my readers and critics.

PART ONE
theory

one
THE TRIUMPH OF JUST WAR THEORY
(AND THE DANGERS OF SUCCESS)
(2002)

Some political theories die and go to heaven; some, I hope, die and go to hell. But some have a long life in this world, a history most often of service to the powers-that-be, but also, sometimes, an oppositionist history. The theory of just war began in the service of the powers. At least that is how I interpret Augustine's achievement: he replaced the radical refusal of Christian pacifists with the active ministry of the Christian soldier. Now pious Christians could fight on behalf of the worldly city, for the sake of imperial peace (in this case, literally, *pax Romana*); but they had to fight justly, only for the sake of peace, and always, Augustine insisted, with a downcast demeanor, without anger or lust.[1] Seen from the perspective of primitive Christianity, this account of just war was simply an excuse, a way of making war morally and religiously possible. And that was indeed the function of the theory. But its defenders would have said, and I am inclined to agree, that it made war possible in a world where war was, sometimes, necessary.

From the beginning, the theory had a critical edge: soldiers (or, at least, their officers) were supposed to refuse to fight in wars of conquest and to oppose or abstain from the standard military practices of rape and pillage after the battle was won. But just war was a worldly theory, in every sense of that term, and it continued to serve worldly interests against Christian radicalism. It is important to note, though, that Christian radicalism had more than one version: it could be expressed in a pacifist rejection of war, but it could also be expressed in war itself, in the religiously driven crusade. Augustine opposed the first of these; the medieval scholastics, following in Aquinas's footsteps, set themselves against the second. The classic statement is Vitoria's: "Difference of religion cannot be a cause of just war." For centuries, from the time of the Crusades to the religious wars of the Reformation years, many of the priests and preachers of Christian Europe, many lords and barons (and even a few kings), had been committed to the legitimacy of using military force against unbelievers: they had their own version of *jihad*. Vitoria claimed, by contrast, that "the sole and only just cause for waging war is when harm has been inflicted."[2] Just war was an argument of the religious center against pacifists, on the one side, and holy warriors, on the other, and because of its enemies (and even though its proponents were theologians), it took shape as a secular theory — which is simply another way of describing its worldliness.

So the rulers of this world embraced the theory, and did not fight a single war without describing it, or hiring intellectuals to describe it, as a war for peace and justice. Most often, of course, this description was hypocritical: the tribute that vice pays to virtue. But the need to pay the tribute opens those who pay it to the criticism of the virtuous — that is, of the brave and virtuous, of whom there have been only a few (but one could also say: at least a few). I will cite one heroic moment, from the history of the academic world: sometime around 1520, the faculty of the University of Salamanca met in solemn assembly and voted that the Spanish conquest of Central America was a violation of natural law and an unjust war.[3] I have not been able to learn anything about the subsequent fate of the good professors. Certainly, there were not many moments like that one, but what happened at Salamanca suggests that just war never lost its critical edge. The theory provided worldly reasons for going to war, but the reasons were limited — and they had to be worldly. Converting the Aztecs to Christianity was not a just cause; nor was seizing the gold of the Americas or enslaving its inhabitants.

Writers like Grotius and Pufendorf incorporated just war theory into international law, but the rise of the modern state and the legal (and philosophical) acceptance of state sovereignty pushed the theory into the background. Now the political foreground was occupied by people we can think of as Machiavellian princes, hard men (and sometimes women), driven by "reason of state," who did what (they said) they had to do. Worldly prudence triumphed over worldly justice; realism over what was increasingly disparaged as naive idealism. The princes of the world continued to defend their wars, using the language of international law, which was also, at least in part, the language of just war. But the defenses were marginal to the enterprise, and I suspect that it was the least important of the state's intellectuals who put them forward. States claimed a right to fight whenever their rulers deemed it necessary, and the rulers took sovereignty to mean that no one could judge their decisions. They not only fought when they wanted; they fought how they wanted, returning to the old Roman maxim that held war to be a lawless activity: *inter arma silent leges* — which, again, was taken to mean that there was no law above or beyond the decrees of the state; conventional restraints on the conduct of war could always be overridden for the sake of victory.[4] Arguments about justice were treated as a kind of moralizing, inappropriate to the anarchic conditions of international society. For this world, just war was not worldly enough.

In the 1950s and early 1960s, when I was in graduate school, realism was the reigning doctrine in the field of "international relations." The standard reference was not to justice but to interest. Moral argument was against the rules of the discipline as it was commonly practiced, although a few writers defended interest as the new morality.[5] There were many political scientists in those years who preened themselves as modern Machiavellis and dreamed of whispering in the ear of the prince; and a certain number of them, enough to stimulate the ambition of the others, actually got to whisper. They practiced being cool and tough-minded; they taught the princes, who did not always need to be taught, how to get results through the calculated application of force. Results were understood in terms of "the national interest," which was the objectively determined sum of power and wealth here and now plus the probability of future power and wealth. More of both was almost always taken to be better; only a few writers argued for the acceptance of prudential limits; moral limits were, as I remember those years, never discussed. Just war theory was relegated to religion departments, theological seminaries, and a few Catholic universities. And even in those places, isolated as they were from the political world, the theory was pressed toward realist positions; perhaps for the sake of self-preservation, its advocates surrendered something of its critical edge.

Vietnam changed all this, although it took a while for the change to register at the theoretical level. What happened first occurred in the realm of practice. The war became a subject of political debate; it was widely opposed, mostly by people on the left. These were people heavily influenced by Marxism; they also spoke a language of interest; they shared with the princes and professors of American politics a disdain for moralizing. And yet the experience of the war pressed them toward moral argument. Of course, the war in their eyes was radically imprudent; it could not be won; its costs, even if Americans thought only of themselves, were much too high; it was an imperialist adventure unwise even for the imperialists; it set the United States against the cause of national liberation, which would alienate it from the Third World (and significant parts of the First). But these claims failed utterly to express the feelings of most of the war's opponents, feelings that had to do with the systematic exposure of Vietnamese civilians to the violence of American war-making. Almost against its will, the left fell into morality. All of us in the antiwar camp suddenly began talking the language of just war — though we did not know that that was what we were doing.

It may seem odd to recall the '60s in this way, since today the left seems all too quick to make moral arguments, even absolutist moral arguments. But this description of the contemporary left seems to me mistaken. A certain kind of politicized, instrumental, and highly selective moralizing is indeed increasingly common among leftist writers, but this is not serious moral argument. It is not what we learned, or ought to have learned, from the Vietnam years. What happened then was that people on the left, and many others too, looked for a common moral language. And what was most available was the language of just war. We were, all of us, a bit rusty, unaccustomed to speaking in public about morality. The realist ascendancy had robbed us of the very words that we needed, which we slowly reclaimed: aggression, intervention, just cause, self-defense, noncombatant immunity, proportionality, prisoners of war, civilians, double effect, terrorism, war crimes. And we came to understand that these words had meanings. Of course, they could be used instrumentally; that is always true of political and moral terms. But if we attended to their meanings, we found ourselves involved in a discussion that had its own structure. Like characters in a novel, concepts in a theory shape the narrative or the argument in which they figure.

Once the war was over, just war became an academic subject; now political scientists and philosophers discovered the theory; it was written about in the journals and taught in the universities — and also in the (American) military academies and war colleges. A small group of Vietnam veterans played a major role in making the discipline of morality central to the military curriculum.[6] They had bad memories. They welcomed just war theory precisely because it was in their eyes a critical theory. It is, in fact, doubly critical — of war's occasions and its conduct. I suspect that the veterans were most concerned with the second of these. It is not only that they wanted to avoid anything like the My Lai massacre in future wars; they wanted, like professional soldiers everywhere, to distinguish their profession from mere butchery. And because of their Vietnam experience, they believed that this had to be done systematically; it required not only a code but also a theory. Once upon a time, I suppose, aristocratic honor had grounded the military code; in a more democratic and egalitarian age, the code had to be defended with arguments.

And so we argued. The discussions and debates were wide-ranging even if, once the war was over, they were mostly academic. It is easy to forget how large the academic world is in the United States: there are millions of students and tens of thousands of professors. So a lot of people were involved, future citizens and army officers, and the theory was mostly presented, though this presentation was also disputed, as a manual for war-time criticism. Our cases and examples were drawn from Vietnam and were framed to invite criticism. Here was a war that we should never have fought, and that we fought badly, brutally, as if there were no moral limits. So it became, retrospectively, an occasion for drawing a line — and for committing ourselves to the moral casuistry necessary to determine the precise location of the line. Ever since Pascal's brilliant denunciation, casuistry has had a bad name among moral philosophers; it is commonly taken to be excessively permissive, not so much an application as a relaxation of the moral rules. When we looked back at the Vietnamese cases, however, we were more likely to deny permission than to grant it, insisting again and again that what had been done should not have been done.

But there was another feature of Vietnam that gave the moral critique of the war special force: it was a war that we lost, and the brutality with which we fought the war almost certainly contributed to our defeat. In a war for "hearts and minds," rather than for land and resources, justice turns out to be a key to victory. So just war theory looked once again like the worldly doctrine that it is. And here, I think, is the deepest cause of the theory's contemporary triumph: there are now reasons of state for fighting justly. One might almost say that justice has become a military necessity.

There were probably earlier wars in which the deliberate killing of civilians, and also the common military carelessness about killing civilians, proved to be counterproductive. The Boer war is a likely example. But for us, Vietnam was the first war in which the practical value of *jus in bello* became apparent. To be sure, the "Vietnam syndrome" is generally taken to reflect a different lesson: that we should not fight wars that are unpopular at home and to which we are unwilling to commit the resources necessary for victory. But there was in fact another lesson, connected to but not the same as the "syndrome": that we should not fight wars about whose justice we are doubtful, and that once we are engaged we have to fight justly so as not to antagonize the civilian population, whose political support is necessary to a military victory. In Vietnam, the relevant civilians were the Vietnamese themselves; we lost the war when we lost their "hearts and minds." But this idea about the need for civilian support has turned out to be both variable and expansive: modern warfare requires the support of different civilian populations, extending beyond the population immediately at risk. Still, a moral regard for civilians at risk is critically important in winning wider support for the war . . . for any modern war. I will call this the usefulness of morality. Its wide acknowledgement is something radically new in military history.

Hence the odd spectacle of George Bush (the elder), during the Persian Gulf war, talking like a just war theorist.[7] Well, not quite: for Bush's speeches and press conferences displayed an old American tendency, which his son has inherited, to confuse just wars and crusades, as if a war can be just only when the forces of good are arrayed against the forces of evil. But Bush also seemed to understand — and this was a constant theme of American military spokesmen — that war is properly a war of armies, a combat between combatants, from which the civilian population should be shielded. I do not believe that the bombing of Iraq in 1991 met just war standards; shielding civilians would certainly have excluded the destruction of electricity networks and water purification plants. Urban infrastructure, even if it is necessary to modern war-making, is also necessary to civilian existence in a modern city, and it is morally defined by this second feature.[8] Still, American strategy in the Gulf war was the result of a compromise between what justice would have required and the unrestrained bombing of previous wars; taken overall, targeting was far more limited and selective than it had been, for example, in Korea or Vietnam. The reasons for the limits were complicated: in part, they reflected a commitment to the Iraqi people (which turned out not to be very strong), in the hope that the Iraqis would repudiate the war and overthrow the regime that began it; in part, they reflected the political necessities of the coalition that made the war possible. Those necessities were shaped in turn by the media coverage of the war — that is, by the immediate access of the media to the battle and of people the world over to the media. Bush and his generals believed that these people would not tolerate a slaughter of civilians, and they were probably right (but what it might mean for them not to tolerate something was and is fairly unclear). Hence, although many of the countries whose support was crucial to the war's success were not democracies, bombing policy was dictated in important ways by the demos.

This will continue to be true: the media are omnipresent, and the whole world is watching. War has to be different in these circumstances. But does this mean that it has to be more just or only that it has to look most just, that it has to be described, a little more persuasively than in the past, in the language of justice? The triumph of just war theory is clear enough; it is amazing how readily military spokesmen during the Kosovo and Afghanistan wars used its categories, telling a causal story that justified the war and providing accounts of the battles that emphasized the restraint with which they were being fought. The arguments (and rationalizations) of the past were very different; they commonly came from outside the armed forces — from clerics, lawyers, and professors, not from generals — and they commonly lacked specificity and detail. But what does the use of these categories, these just and moral words, signify?

Perhaps naively, I am inclined to say that justice has become, in all Western countries, one of the tests that any proposed military strategy or tactic has to meet — only one of the tests and not the most important one, but this still gives just war theory a place and standing that it never had before. It is easier now than it ever was to imagine a general saying, "No, we can't do that; it would cause too many civilian deaths; we have to find another way." I am not sure that there are many generals who talk like that, but imagine for a moment that there are; imagine that strategies are evaluated morally as well as militarily; that civilian deaths are minimized; that new technologies are designed to avoid or limit collateral damage, and that these technologies are actually effective in achieving their intended purpose. Moral theory has been incorporated into war-making as a real constraint on when and how wars are fought. This picture is, remember, imaginary, but it is also partly true; and it makes for a far more interesting argument than the more standard claim that the triumph of just war is pure hypocrisy. The triumph is real: what then is left for theorists and philosophers to do?

This question is sufficiently present in our consciousness that one can watch people trying to respond. There are two responses that I want to describe and criticize. The first comes from what might be called the postmodern left, which does not claim that affirmations of justice are hypocritical, since hypocrisy implies standards, but rather that there are no standards, no possible objective use of the categories of just war theory.[9] Politicians and generals who adopt the categories are deluding themselves —

though no more so than the theorists who developed the categories in the first place. Maybe new technologies kill fewer people, but there is no point in arguing about who those people are and whether or not killing them is justified. No agreement about justice, or about guilt or innocence, is possible. This view is summed up in a line that speaks to our immediate situation: "One man's terrorist is another man's freedom fighter." On this view, there is nothing for theorists and philosophers to do but choose sides, and there is no theory or principle that can guide their choice. But this is an impossible position, for it holds that we cannot recognize, condemn, and actively oppose the murder of innocent people.

A second response is to take the moral need to recognize, condemn and oppose very seriously and then to raise the theoretical ante — that is, to strengthen the constraints that justice imposes on warfare. For theorists who pride themselves on living, so to speak, at the critical edge, this is an obvious and understandable response. For many years, we have used the theory of just war to criticize American military actions, and now it has been taken over by the generals and is being used to explain and justify those actions. Obviously, we must resist. The easiest way to resist is to make noncombatant immunity into a stronger and stronger rule, until it is something like an absolute rule: all killing of civilians is (something close to) murder; therefore any war that leads to the killing of civilians is unjust; therefore every war is unjust. So pacifism reemerges from the very heart of the theory that was originally meant to replace it. This is the strategy adopted, most recently, by many opponents of the Afghanistan war. The protest marches on American campuses featured banners proclaiming, "Stop the Bombing!" and the argument for stopping was very simple (and obviously true): bombing endangers and kills civilians. The marchers did not seem to feel that anything more had to be said.

Since I believe that war is still, sometimes, necessary, this seems to me a bad argument and, more generally, a bad response to the triumph of just war theory. It sustains the critical role of the theory vis-à-vis war generally, but it denies the theory the critical role it has always claimed, which is internal to the business of war and requires critics to attend closely to what soldiers try to do and what they try not to do. The refusal to make distinctions of this kind, to pay attention to strategic and tactical choices, suggests a doctrine of radical suspicion. This is the radicalism of people who do not expect to exercise power or use force, ever, and who are not prepared to make the judgments that this exercise and use require. By contrast, just war theory, even when it demands a strong critique of particular acts of war, is the doctrine of people who do expect to exercise power and use force. We might think of it as a doctrine of radical responsibility, because it holds political and military leaders responsible, first of all, for the well-being of their own people, but also for the well-being of innocent men and women on the other side. Its proponents set themselves against those who will not think realistically about the defense of the country they live in and also against those who refuse to recognize the humanity of their opponents. They insist that there are things that it is morally impermissible to do even to the enemy. They also insist, however, that fighting itself cannot be morally impermissible. A just war is meant to be, and has to be, a war that it is possible to fight.

But there is another danger posed by the triumph of just war theory — not the radical relativism and the near absolutism that I have just described, but rather a certain softening of the critical mind, a truce between theorists and soldiers. If intellectuals are often awed and silenced by political leaders who invite them to dinner, how much more so by generals who talk their language? And if the generals are actually fighting just wars, if *inter arma* the laws speak, what point is there in anything we can say? In fact, however, our role has not changed all that much. We still have to insist that war is a morally dubious and difficult activity. Even if we (in the West) have fought just wars in the Gulf, in Kosovo, and in Afghanistan, that is no guarantee, not even a useful indication, that our next war will be just. And even if the recognition of noncombatant immunity has become militarily necessary, it still conflicts with other, more pressing, necessities. Justice still needs to be defended; decisions about when and how to fight require constant scrutiny, exactly as they always have.

At the same time, we have to extend our account of "when and how" to cover the new strategies, the new technologies, and the new politics of a global age. Old ideas may not fit the emerging reality: the "war against terrorism," to take the most current example, requires a kind of international cooperation that is as radically undeveloped in theory as it is in practice. We should welcome military officers into the theoretical argument; they will make it a better argument than it would be if no one but professors took an interest. But we cannot leave the argument to them. As the old saying goes, war is too important to be left to the generals; just war even more so. The ongoing critique of warmaking is a centrally important democratic activity.

Let me, then, suggest two issues, raised by our most recent wars, that require the critical edge of justice.

First, risk-free war-making. I have heard it said that this is a necessary feature of humanitarian interventions like the Kosovo war: soldiers defending humanity, in contrast to soldiers defending their own country and their fellow-citizens, will not risk their lives; or, their political leaders will not dare to ask them to risk their lives. Hence the rescue of people in desperate trouble, the objects of massacre or ethnic cleansing, is only possible if risk-free war is possible.[10] But, obviously, it is possible: wars can be fought from a great distance with bombs and missiles aimed very precisely (compared with the radical imprecision of such weapons only a few decades ago) at the forces carrying out the killings and deportations. And the soldier-technicians aiming these weapons are, in all the recent cases, largely invulnerable to counterattack. There is no principle of just war theory that bars this kind of warfare. So long as they can aim accurately at military targets, soldiers have every right to fight from a safe distance. And what commander, committed to his or her own soldiers, would not choose to fight in this way whenever it was possible? In his reflections on rebellion, Albert Camus argues that one cannot kill unless one is prepared to die.[11] But that argument does not seem to apply to soldiers in battle, where the whole point is to kill while avoiding getting killed. And yet there is a wider sense in which Camus is right.

Just war theorists have not, to my knowledge, discussed this question, but we obviously need to do so [see the essay on Kosovo (Chapter 7) for a brief discussion]. Massacre and ethnic cleansing commonly take place on the ground. The awful work might be done with bombs and poison gas delivered from the air, but in Bosnia, Kosovo, Rwanda, East Timor, and Sierra Leone, the weapons were rifles, machetes, and clubs; the killing and terrorizing of the population were carried out from close up. And a risk-free intervention undertaken from far away — especially if it promises to be effective in the long run — is likely to cause an immediate speed-up on the ground. This can be stopped only if the intervention itself shifts to the ground, and this shift seems to be morally necessary. The aim of the intervention, after all, is to rescue people in trouble, and fighting on the ground, in the case as I have described it, is what rescue requires. But then it is no longer risk-free. Why would anyone undertake it?

In fact, risks of this sort are a common feature of *jus in bello*, and while there are many examples of soldiers unwilling to accept them, there are also many examples of their acceptance. The principle is this: when it is our action that puts innocent people at risk, even if the action is justified, we are bound to do what we can to reduce those risks, even if this involves risks to our own soldiers. If we are bombing military targets in a just war, and there are civilians living near these targets, we have to adjust our bombing policy — by flying at lower altitudes, say — so as to minimize the risks we impose on civilians. Of course, it is legitimate to balance the risks; we cannot require our pilots to fly suicidal missions. They have to be, as Camus suggests, prepared to die, but that is consistent with taking measures to safeguard their lives. How the balance gets worked out is something that has to be debated in each case. But what is not permissible, it seems to me, is what NATO did in the Kosovo war, where its leaders declared in advance that they would not send ground forces into battle, whatever happened inside Kosovo once the air war began. Responsibility for the intensified Serbian campaign against Kosovar civilians, which was the immediate consequence of the air war, belongs no doubt to the Serbian government and army.

They were to blame. But this was at the same time a foreseeable result of our action, and insofar as we did nothing to prepare for this result, or to deal with it, we were blameworthy too. We imposed risks on others and refused to accept them for ourselves, even when that acceptance was necessary to help the others.[12]

The second issue concerns war's endings. On the standard view, a just war (precisely because it is not a crusade) should end with the restoration of the status quo ante. The paradigm case is a war of aggression, which ends justly when the aggressor has been defeated, his attack repulsed, the old boundaries restored. Perhaps this is not quite enough for a just conclusion: the victim state might deserve reparations from the aggressor state, so that the damage the aggressor's forces inflicted can be repaired — a more extensive understanding of restoration, but restoration still. And perhaps the peace treaty should include new security arrangements, of a sort that did not exist before the war, so that the status quo will be more stable in the future. But that is as far as the rights of victims go; the theory as it was commonly understood did not extend to any radical reconstitution of the enemy state, and international law, with its assumptions about sovereignty, would have regarded any imposed change of regime as a new act of aggression. What happened after World War II in both Germany and Japan was something quite new in the history of war, and the legitimacy of occupation and political reconstitution is still debated, even by theorists and lawyers who regard the treatment of the Nazi regime, at least, as justified. Thus, as the Gulf war drew to a close in 1991, there was little readiness to march on Baghdad and replace the government of Saddam Hussein, despite the denunciation of that government in the lead-up to the war as Nazi-like in character. There were, of course, both military and geo-political arguments against continuing the war once the attack on Kuwait had been repulsed, but there was also an argument from justice: that even if Iraq "needed" a new government, that need could only be met by the Iraqi people themselves. A government imposed by foreign armies would never be accepted as the product of, or the future agent of, self-determination.[13]

The World War II examples, however, argue against this last claim. If the imposed government is democratic and moves quickly to open up the political arena and to organize elections, it may erase the memory of its own imposition (hence the difference between the western and eastern regimes in post-war Germany). In any case, humanitarian intervention radically shifts the argument about endings, because now the war is from the beginning an effort to change the regime that is responsible for the inhumanity. This can be done by supporting secession, as the Indians did in what is now Bangladesh; or by expelling a dictator, as the Tanzanians did to Uganda's Idi Amin; or by creating a new government, as the Vietnamese did in Cambodia. In East Timor, more recently, the U.N. organized a referendum on secession and then worked to set up a new government. Had there been, as there should have been, an intervention in Rwanda, it would certainly have aimed at replacing the Hutu Power regime. Justice would have required the replacement. But what kind of justice is this? Who are its agents, and what rules govern their actions?

As the Rwandan example suggests, most states do not want to take on this kind of responsibility, and when they do take it on, for whatever political reasons, they do not want to submit themselves to a set of moral rules. In Cambodia, the Vietnamese shut down the killing fields, which was certainly a good thing to do, but they then went on to set up a satellite government, keyed to their own interests, which never won legitimacy either within or outside of Cambodia and brought no closure to the country's internal conflicts. Legitimacy and closure are the two criteria against which we can test war's endings. Both of them are likely to require, in almost all the humanitarian intervention cases, something more than the restoration of the status quo ante — which gave rise, after all, to the crisis that prompted the intervention. Legitimacy and closure, however, are hard tests to meet. The problems have to do in part with strategic interests, as in the Vietnamese-Cambodian case. But material interests also figure in a major way: remaking a government is an expensive business; it requires a significant commitment of resources — and the benefits are largely speculative and nonmaterial. Yet we can still point to the usefulness of morality in cases like these. A successful and extended intervention brings benefits of an important kind: not only gratitude and friendship, but an increment of peace and stability in a world where the insufficiency of both is costly — and not only to its immediate victims. Still, any particular country will always have good reasons to refuse to bear the costs of these benefits; or it will take on the burden, and then find reasons to perform badly. So we still need justice's critical edge.

The argument about endings is similar to the argument about risk: once we have acted in ways that have significant negative consequences for other people (even if there are also positive consequences), we cannot just walk away. Imagine a humanitarian intervention that ends with the massacres stopped and the murderous regime overthrown; but the country is devastated, the economy in ruins, the people hungry and afraid; there is neither law nor order nor any effective authority. The forces that inter-

vened did well, but they are not finished. How can this be? Is it
the price of doing well that you acquire responsibilities to do well
again . . . and again? The work of the virtuous is never finished. It
does not seem fair. But in the real world, not only of international
politics, but also of ordinary morality, this is the ways things work
(though virtue, of course, is never so uncomplicated). Consider
the Afghan-Russian war: the American government intervened
in a major way, fighting by proxy, and eventually won a big victory: the Russians were forced to withdraw. This was the last
battle of the cold war. The American intervention was undoubtedly driven by geopolitical and strategic motives; the conviction
that the Afghan struggle was a war of national liberation against a
repressive regime may have played a part in motivating the people who carried it out, but the allies they found in Afghanistan
had a very restricted idea of liberation.[14] When the war was over,
Afghanistan was left in a state of anarchy and ruin. At that point,
the Americans walked away and were certainly wrong, politically
and morally wrong, to do so; the Russians withdrew and were
right to do so. We had acted (relatively) well, that is, in support of
what was probably the vast majority of the Afghan people, and
yet we were bound to continue acting well; the Russians had
acted badly and were off the hook; even if they owed the Afghan
people material aid (reparations), no one wanted them engaged
again in Afghan affairs. This sounds anomalous, and yet I think it
is an accurate account of the distribution of responsibility. But we
need a better understanding of how this works and why it works
the way it does, a theory of justice-in-endings that engages the
actual experience of humanitarian (and other) interventions, so
that countries fighting in wars like these know what their responsibilities will be if they win. It would also help if there was, what

there is not yet, an international agency that could stipulate and even enforce these responsibilities.

This theory of justice-in-endings will have to include a description of legitimate occupations, regime changes, and protectorates—and also, obviously, a description of illegitimate and immoral activity in all these areas. This combination is what just war has always been about: it makes actions and operations that are morally problematic *possible* by constraining their occasions and regulating their conduct. When the constraints are accepted, the actions and operations are justified, and the theorist of just war has to say that, even if he sounds like an apologist for the powers-that-be. When they are not accepted, when the brutalities of war or its aftermath are unconstrained, he has to say that, even if he is called a traitor and an enemy of the people.

It is important not to get stuck in either mode—defense or critique. Indeed, just war theory requires that we maintain our commitment to both modes at the same time. In this sense, just war is like good government: there is a deep and permanent tension between the adjective and the noun, but no necessary contradiction between them. When reformers come to power and make government better (less corrupt, say), we have to be able to acknowledge the improvement. And when they hold on to power for too long, and imitate their predecessors, we have to be ready to criticize their behavior. Just war theory is not an apology for any particular war, and it is not a renunciation of war itself. It is designed to sustain a constant scrutiny and an immanent critique. We still need that, even when generals sound like theorists, and I am sure that we always will.

TWO KINDS OF MILITARY RESPONSIBILITY
(1980)

In writing about military responsibility, I shall try to avoid all reference to questions of free will, intentionality, and the theory of action. I will address instead what I take to be a very difficult, practical problem in our understanding of military responsibility and in our enforcement of it.

It is one of the purposes of any institutional hierarchy, and most especially of the bureaucratic or military chain of command, to resolve questions of responsibility. Who is responsible to whom, and for what? That is what the organizational chart is supposed to show. Once an official or a soldier locates himself on the chart, or in the chain of command, he ought to know exactly who his superiors are and who his subordinates are and what they rightly can expect of him.

Let us consider now the hierarchical position of a middle-level officer in time of war, a field commander responsible for making tactical decisions. He has a twofold responsibility that can be described in simple directional terms. First, he is responsible *upward* — to his military commanders and then through the highest of them, the commander-in-chief, to the sovereign people, whose "officer" he properly is and to whose collective safety and protection he is pledged. His obligation is to win the battles that he fights or, rather, to do his best to win, obeying the legal orders of his immediate superiors, fitting his own decisions into the larger strategic plan, accepting onerous but necessary tasks, seeking collective success rather than individual glory. He is responsible for assignments unperformed or badly performed and for all avoidable defeats. And he is responsible up the chain to each of his superiors in turn and ultimately to the ordinary citizens of his country who are likely to suffer for his failures.

But there are other people likely to suffer for his failures and, often enough, for his successes too — namely, the soldiers that he commands. And so he is also responsible *downward* — to each and every one of them. His soldiers are in one sense the instruments with which he is supposed to win victories, but they are also men and women whose lives, because they are his to use, are also in his care. He is bound to minimize the risks his soldiers must face, to fight carefully and prudently, and to avoid wasting their lives, that is, not to persist in battles that cannot be won, not to seek victories whose costs overwhelm their military value, and so on. And his soldiers have every right to expect all this of him and to blame him for every sort of omission, evasion, carelessness, and recklessness that endangers their lives.

Now these two sets of responsibilities, up and down the chain of command, together constitute what I shall call the hierarchical responsibilities of the officer. I assume that there can be tensions between the two, and that these tensions are commonly experienced in the field. They have to do with the regret that officers must feel that the primary instruments with which they fight are human beings, to whom they are morally connected. But I don't think that there can be direct conflicts and contradictions between upward and downward responsibility. For there is only one hierarchy; a single chain of command; in principle, at least, a singular conception of victory; and finally a commitment up and down the chain to win that victory. It cannot be the case, then, that a commander who sacrifices his soldiers, so long as he does the best he can to minimize the extent of the sacrifice, does anything that he does not have a right to do. Whenever I read about trench warfare in World War I, I can hardly avoid the sense that the officers who sent so many soldiers to their deaths for so little gain in one attack after another were literally mad. But if that is so, the madness was reiterated at every level of the hierarchy — up to the level where political leaders stubbornly refused every compromise that might have ended the war. And so officers further down, at least those who carefully prepared for each successive attack and called off the attacks when it was clear that they had failed, did not act unjustly, while officers who were neither careful in advance nor willing later on to admit failure can readily be condemned for violating their hierarchical responsibilities. And all this is true even if the war as a whole, or the continuation of the war, was unjustified, and even if this way of fighting it was insane. I do not think it can ever be impermissible for an officer to send his soldiers into battle: that is what he is for and that is what they are for.

But the case is very different, I think, when we come to consider the officer's responsibilities for the civilian casualties of the battles he fights. As a moral agent, he is also responsible *outward* — to all those people whose lives his activities affect. This is a responsibility that we all have, since we are all moral agents, and it is, at least in the first instance, non-hierarchical in character. No organizational chart can possibly determine our duties or obligations to other people generally. What we ought to do when we face outward is determined by divine or natural law, or by a conception of human rights, or by a utilitarian calculation in which everyone's interest, and not only those up and down the hierarchy, must be counted. However that determination works out in particular cases, it is clear that the duties or obligations of moral agents may well conflict with the demands of the organizations they serve. In the case of a state or army at war, the conflict is often dramatic and painful. The civilians whose lives are put at risk are commonly neither superiors nor subordinates; they have no place in the hierarchy. The injuries done to them can be and often are wrongful, and, what is most important, they can be wrongful (so I want to argue) even if they are done in the course of military operations carried out in strict accordance with the precepts of hierarchical responsibility.

The distinction that I have drawn between the two kinds of military responsibility — the hierarchical and non-hierarchical — is, of course, too sharp and neat. There has been an effort of long-standing to incorporate the second of these into the first, that is, to make soldiers answerable to their officers for crimes committed against the civilian population and to make officers answerable to their superiors (and even to their enemies) for the crimes committed by their soldiers. This is a commendable effort, and I don't want to underestimate its value. But I think it is fair to say that it has not been very successful. It works best with regard to those crimes against civilians that are, so to speak, superfluous to the war effort as a whole — and best of all when the superfluousness is a matter of indiscipline. The ordinary desire of a commander to retain command of his soldiers will lead him to repress indiscipline as best he can and to hold his soldiers to a high and consistent standard of conduct. At least, it should do that: for the best soldiers, the best fighting men, do not loot and rape. Similarly, the best soldiers do not wantonly kill civilians. Massacres of the My Lai sort are most often the result of fear and rage, and neither of these emotions makes for the maximum efficiency of the "war machine" that soldiers sometimes ought to be. Like looting and rape, massacre is militarily as well as morally reprehensible, for it represents a loss of control as well as a criminal act, and so it is more or less easily dealt with in hierarchical terms.

I say "more or less easily" because even superfluous injury often takes place within a context of command and obedience: My Lai is again an example. What we require of soldiers in that situation is that they refuse the orders — the illegal or immoral orders — of their immediate superior. That refusal does not constitute a denial of or a rebellion against the military hierarchy. It is best understood as an appeal up the chain of command over a superior officer to the superiors of that superior officer. Given the structure of the chain and its purposes, any such appeal is problematic and difficult, a matter of considerable strain for the individual who undertakes it. He is still operating, however, within the conventions of hierarchical responsibility.

But when the killing of civilians is plausibly connected to some military purpose, those conventions seem to provide no recourse at all. Neither in the case of direct and intended killing, as in siege warfare or terror bombing, nor in the case of incidental and unintended killing, as in the bombardment of a military target that results in a disproportionate number of civilian deaths, is there any effective responsibility up or down the hierarchy. I don't mean that individuals are not responsible for such killings, only that there is no hierarchical way of holding them responsible or at least no *effective* hierarchical way of so holding them. Nor is there any way of pointing to the organizational chart and explaining to whom responsibility can be attributed. For in these cases, the hierarchy seems to be working very much as it was meant to work. Here are victories, let's assume, victories won at a wonderfully low cost to the soldiers who win them. Their commanding officer can look up and down the hierarchy and feel good about what he is doing.

I should make that last point more strongly: the officer can look up and down the hierarchy and feel that he is doing what he ought to be doing. He is pursuing victory with all the means at his disposal, which is what his superiors want him to do, and what we, as members of the sovereign people, want him to do. And he is pursuing victory at the least possible cost to his own soldiers, which is no doubt what they want him to do. And so he meets the moral requirements of his hierarchical position. It is worth noticing that these are exactly the moral requirements that President Truman claimed to be meeting when he approved the use of the atomic bomb on Hiroshima. He made his decision, so he told us in his radio broadcast of 9 August 1945, in order to end the war and to save American lives. Those two purposes, he seemed to assume, exhausted his responsibilities. And that is not an implausible assumption if we think of him only as the commander-in-chief of a nation and an army at war.

We can say, I think, that Truman's argument does address the full range of his hierarchical, but not the full range of his moral, responsibilities. But he might have gone on to argue — though it is important to say that he did not go on to argue — that he knew himself to be responsible as a human being and a moral agent for all the civilian deaths caused by his decision. But, he might still have said, his responsibility to the American people as a whole and to individual American soldiers took precedence over his responsibility for Japanese civilians because of his hierarchical position. And any officer further down the hierarchy could make the same argument: that his oath of office and his immediate bond to his soldiers determine what he ought to do, whatever other considerations he might acknowledge.

Now, if this argument encompassed the whole truth, then the killing of civilians, so long as it was connected to some military purpose, could no more conflict with hierarchical responsibilities than the different sorts of hierarchical responsibilities could conflict with one another. Civilians would be subordinated, exactly as soldiers are, to military purposiveness, and then further subordinated to the safety and preservation of our own soldiers (and the other side would subordinate civilians in exactly the same way). In effect, they would be incorporated into the hierarchy at its lowest point and recognized within the system of hierarchical responsibility only when they were needlessly and superfluously attacked. But this incorporation is nothing more than an act of conquest and tyranny. For the civilians whose lives are at stake are citizens of other countries who have no place in *this* hierarchy. The middle-level officer that I am considering is not their agent; no legal or bureaucratic procedures make him answerable to them. Nor are they his agents, subject to his command, submitted to his care and protection. Indeed, he sees them only when he looks outward, away from his hierarchical responsibilities. And if he is to recognize them, to attend to their interests and rights, he may well have to turn away from his hierarchical responsibilities and diminish the care and protection he affords to his own soldiers — that is, he may have to impose added risks on the soldiers for the sake of the civilians. The conflict, then, is a real one.

Because the conflict is real, it is vitally important that it be mediated in some institutional form. But I don't know of any easy or obvious way of specifying, let alone of establishing, the appropriate form. Ideally, an army ought to be watched and checked by something like a civilian board of review. But if we think of the place that such boards occupy alongside police departments in some of our major cities, we can immediately see the problems that would arise in the case of an army. For while the board of review represents civilians as potential victims of police neglect or brutality, those same civilians are also the ultimate employers of the police. They elect the mayor who appoints the police chief, and so on. They have a place in the urban chain of command, perhaps a double place, at the top and bottom of the chain. But citizens of other countries have, as I have just argued, no place at all in the chain and no power over the political leaders who appoint army generals. They are potential victims, and that is all they are, and we cannot imagine them effectively represented by any civilian board of review.

They might be represented internationally, by a court like the Nuremberg tribunal after World War II. But it is an interesting feature of the decisions made at Nuremberg and by the associated courts that they did not go very far toward enforcing the non-hierarchical responsibilities of soldiers. Mostly, they worked at the margins of the moral space that I have meant to mark out with that term, condemning individual officers for the killing of hostages, of sailors helpless in the water, and of prisoners of war. But they convicted no one for siege warfare or terror bombing or any form of disregard for civilian lives. In part, this was because these kinds of warfare were by no means peculiar to the Germans. In part, it was because the legal status of these kinds of warfare is at best uncertain. Traditionally, in the laws of war, hierarchical responsibilities have dominated non-hierarchical responsibilities. Recent revisions of the law, at Geneva in 1949 and again in 1978, have not produced any radical challenge to that domination.

I must conclude, therefore, that the non-hierarchical responsibilities of officers have, at this moment, no satisfactory institutional form. Nor are they likely to have until we include them systematically in our understanding of what military office requires. Conceivably, this might be easier to do in an era when so many wars are political wars, fought as much for the loyalty of the civilian population as for control of land and resources. In such a time, one would think, responsibilities outward and upward will often coincide or at least overlap more extensively than in a time of conventional warfare. And then purposive crimes as well as crimes of indiscipline might come under hierarchical scrutiny. But in all times, and in conventional as well as political wars, we ought to require of officers that they attend to the value of civilian lives, and we should refuse to honor officers who fail to do that, even if they win great victories thereby.

"The soldier," wrote General Douglas MacArthur at the time of the Yamashita trial, ". . . is charged with the protection of the weak and unarmed. It is the very essence and reason of his being . . . [a] sacred trust." Now, I suppose that is overstated. The "reason" of soldiering is victory, and the "reason" of victory is the protection of one's own people, not of other people. But the others are there — the ordinary citizens of enemy and of neutral states — and we are not superior beings who can reduce our risks by slaughtering them: certainly soldiers cannot do that. The lives of the others may or may not be a sacred trust, but they are an ordinary responsibility whenever we act in ways that endanger them. And we must make a place for that responsibility within the more specialized and more easily institutionalized "reasons" of war. Since the most immediate and problematic moral tension is the conflict between outward and downward responsibilities, between responsibilities for enemy civilians and one's own soldiers, this means first of all that we have to insist upon the risks that soldiers must accept and that their officers must require. I cannot detail these risks here with any hope of precision. What is necessary is a certain sensitivity that the chain of command does not ordinarily elicit or impose. No doubt, that sensitivity would make soldiering even harder than it is, and it is already a hard calling. But given the suffering it often produces, it cannot be the purpose of moral philosophy to make it easier.

EMERGENCY ETHICS

(1988)

My subject in this essay is "supreme emergency." The phrase is Winston Churchill's, and it refers to the crisis of British survival during the darkest days of World War II.[1] Supreme emergency is a time for heroic decision, when nations and leaders are measured by the measures they take; but it is also a desperate time, when the measures taken are ones we would avoid if we possibly could. I wish no such time on my own country and my fellow citizens. Let this be a theoretical discussion and an educational exercise. We can test our everyday moral perceptions against an extreme case, and we can ask whether there are useful analogies between historical or hypothetical extremity and what passes today for normality. I suggest a certain wariness about the exercise. As hard cases make bad law, so supreme emergencies put morality itself at risk. We need to be careful.

More than a decade ago, in *Just and Unjust Wars*, I worked out an argument about supreme emergency that was driven by Churchill's account of the British crisis and by my own memory of and reflection on the struggle against Nazism.[2] I took the years 1940 and 1941, when a Nazi victory in Europe seemed frighteningly close, as my model. A supreme emergency exists when our deepest values and our collective survival are in imminent danger, and that was the situation in those years. Can moral constraints have any hold upon us at such a time? What can and what should political leaders do when confronting danger on that scale? I gave a philosophically provocative and paradoxical answer to those questions. I argued, first, that the constraints did still have a hold on us; and second, that political leaders could do whatever was required to meet the danger. There are no moments in human history that are not governed by moral rules; the human world is a world of limitation, and moral limits are never suspended — the way we might, for example, suspend *habeas corpus* in a time of civil war. But there are moments when the rules can be and perhaps have to be overridden. They have to be overridden precisely because they have not been suspended. And overriding the rules leaves guilt behind, as a recognition of the enormity of what we have done and a commitment not to make our actions into an easy precedent for the future.

The example in my mind when I first made that argument was the British decision to bomb German cities — specifically the orders issued to bomber crews in the early 1940s to aim at the city center or at residential areas (that is, not at military bases, factories, shipyards, warehouses, and so on). The intention of the British leaders at that point in the war was to kill and terrorize the civilian population, to attack German morale rather than German military might. I won't rehearse here the technical arguments urged by Bomber Command, which had more to do with civilian housing than with civilian lives — as if the two were separable targets — but those arguments were not entirely straightforward.[3] In order to display the theoretical issue in all its difficulty, it is enough to say flatly that the intention was wrongful, the bombing criminal; its victims were innocent men, women, and children. If soldiers or "munitions workers" were also killed, it was only by accident, a morally defensible side effect of what remains an immoral policy. But if there was no other way of preventing a Nazi triumph, then the immorality — no less immoral, for what else can the deliberate killing of the innocent be? — was also, simultaneously, morally defensible. That is the provocation and the paradox. You can imagine the skepticism with which this account of emergency ethics was greeted, especially in philosophical circles, where even the appearance of internal contradiction is taken (as it should be taken) very seriously.[4] So let me try now to explain the argument.

The doctrine of supreme emergency is a way of maneuvering between two very different and characteristically opposed understandings of morality. The first reflects the absolutism of rights theory, according to which innocent human beings can never be intentionally attacked. Innocence is their shield, and though it is only a verbal shield, a paper shield, no defense at all against bombs and bullets, it is impenetrable to moral argument. The second understanding reflects the radical flexibility of utilitarianism, according to which innocence is only one value that must be weighed against other values in the pursuit of the greatest good of the greatest number.[5] I put the opposition crudely; both rights theory and utilitarianism can be developed in complex ways, so that the opposition I have just described is considerably attenuated. But it is never, I think, wholly abolished. Both these moral understandings have claims upon us, and yet they pull us in different directions. It is sometimes said with reference to domestic politics that we should let the courts worry about rights, while congressmen and presidents (and, I suppose, ordinary citizens when they are choosing congressmen and presidents) should think about the greatest good.[6] But this division of responsibility doesn't work. One has only to look closely at the processes of judicial deliberation and legislative debate to see that the two claims are repeatedly made and repeatedly acknowledged within each. In any case, judicial scrutiny in international politics and especially in wartime is notoriously light, and so the two claims necessarily fasten on the political and military leaders of the nation; otherwise they would have no fastening at all. What is the relative strength of the claims? Neither is strong enough to defeat the other; neither is so weak that we can disregard it. At the risk of philosophical muddle, we must negotiate the middle ground.

Why not opt for absolute rights? I have to begin with absolutism, since it represents a denial of the very existence of anything that might be called "middle ground." Morality is not negotiable. Innocence is inviolable. We may disagree, says the absolutist, over who the innocent people are and how they might be located sociologically, but once we have found them, we have also found the final limits of war-making. To protect the innocent or, at least, to exclude them from deliberate attack, is to act justly. And we must act justly whatever the consequences: *fiat justitia, ruat caelum* (do justice even if the heavens fall). The claim of the moral absolutist is that we acknowledge the true meaning of justice only when we ignore the consequences of acting justly — for justice is literally invaluable, beyond the possibility of estimate or measure. It can't be balanced against anything else; the bookkeeper doesn't exist who could strike such a moral balance. Religious absolutists may believe that God keeps his own accounts; they also believe, however, that human beings are bound by his unqualified prohibitions: "Thou shalt not."

This sense that there are things we must never do, forbidden things, taboos, proscriptions, is very old, perhaps older than anything else in our moral understanding. Rule utilitarianism, though it no doubt captures some of the reasons for moral taboos, fails utterly to explain their power. The prohibitions urged upon us by moral absolutists are in fact the common and inescapable rules of moral life. They are external constraints that have long ago been internalized, so that we know the crimes they name not as acts we want to commit but must not, but rather as acts we don't want to commit. Even more, we want not to commit them (not to be murderers, for example), and this desire commonly gets stronger, not weaker, when troubles begin and we find ourselves pressed to act badly. When we feel this pressure, we also feel, most of us, the need to resist. But can we sustain our resistance even when disaster looms, when the heavens are really about to fall? At that point absolutism represents, it seems to me, a refusal to think about what it means for the heavens to fall. And the history of the twentieth century makes that refusal very hard to justify. How can we, with our principles and prohibitions, stand by and watch the destruction of the moral world in which those principles and prohibitions have their hold? How can we, the opponents of murder, fail to resist the practice of mass murder — even if resistance requires us, as the phrase goes, to get our hands dirty (that is, to become murderers ourselves)?

These are rhetorical questions, but I acknowledge immediately that they don't always elicit the response they seem to ask for. Absolutism is by definition unresponsive, and even someone ready in principle to move away from an absolutist position might well respond skeptically. He or she will remind us of how quick some people are to say that the heavens are falling. At the first sign of trouble, they shout "supreme emergency!" and claim exemption from the moral rules. We should always be reluctant to grant such exemptions, for every exemption is also a concession to those who argue that justice has a price, which may sometimes be too high and which we need not always pay. And then the way is open for utilitarian calculation.

Well, what is wrong with utilitarianism? Jeremy Bentham

designed his doctrine for political leaders, and the design seems to have been successful. Hasn't cost/benefit analysis become the standard form of moral reasoning in the arenas of public life? Isn't this the educational core of most university courses on decision theory and policy choice and, I would guess, on military strategy? We value and respect moral taboos but consign them largely to the private sphere. We expect our leaders to be goal-oriented, and we judge them more by the goals they attain than by the rules they uphold. "When the act accuses, the result excuses."[7] How can we avoid, why should we want to avoid, the kind of reckoning this maxim requires?

The problem is that it's too easy to juggle the figures. Utilitarianism, which was supposed to be the most precise and hard-headed of moral arguments, turns out to be the most speculative and arbitrary. For we have to assign values where there is no agreed valuation, no recognized hierarchy of value, no market mechanism for determining the positive or negative worth of different acts and outcomes. Suppose we agree that justice is not in fact beyond measure, invaluable. Then we have to find some way of measuring it, of fixing, for example, the moral cost of murder. How do we do that? Is the cost eight or twenty-three or seventy-seven? Eight or twenty-three or seventy-seven of what? We have no unit of measurement and we have no common or uniform scale. It's not the case, I suppose, that every valuation is idiosyncratic. We are able, for specific purposes (insurance is the common example), to set a dollar price on a human life — though not on the act of taking a human life; the hire of a hit man isn't a morally acceptable figure. In any case, market values for lives-at-risk rise and fall for morally irrelevant reasons. And in politics and war, cost/benefit analysis has always been highly particularistic and endlessly permissive for each particular. Commonly, what we are calculating is *our* benefit (which we exaggerate) and *their* cost (which we minimize or disregard entirely). Is it plausible to expect them to agree to our calculations?

Those first- and third-person plural pronouns ostensibly have no impact on utilitarian calculation; each and every person is valued in the same way; all utilities are measured as if there were a common scale. But this holds in practice only for men and women whose solidarity counterbalances all conflicts of interest among them. When solidarity collapses, in pure or almost pure adversarial situations — in war, for example — utilitarian calculation is zero-sum, and "we" commonly attach only negative value to "their" utilities. Negative valuation is clearest with regard to enemy soldiers when they are actually engaged in combat, but it is likely to extend (unless it is checked by absolutist prohibitions) across the entire population, first to soldiers who are not actually engaged, then to civilians at work in war-related industries, then to civilians who support the war effort indirectly, then to everyone who supports the supporters and the workers and the soldiers. Finally, no "enemy" life has any positive value; we can attack anyone; even infant deaths bring pain and sorrow to adults and so undermine the enemy's resolve. Of course, we can always juggle the figures and stop short of this horrific conclusion. But it is our sense of moral taboos that makes us want to stop short — and it is only by reflecting on the meaning of innocence and on the rights of the innocent that we can decide where in fact to stop.

So the weaknesses of utilitarianism lead us back to the theory of rights, and it is rights that fix the everyday constraints on war-making (and on all adversarial engagements). But these constraints seem to depend on some minimal fixed values, just as utilitarianism depends on some minimum solidarity of persons. When our deepest values are radically at risk, the constraints lose their grip, and a certain kind of utilitarianism reimposes itself. I call this the utilitarianism of extremity, and I set it against a rights normality. The two together, it seems to me, capture the force of the opposed moral understandings and assign to each its proper place. I can't reconcile the understandings; the opposition remains; it is a feature of our moral reality. There are limits on the conduct of war, and there are moments when we can and perhaps should break through the limits (the limits themselves never disappear). "Supreme emergency" describes those rare moments when the negative value that we assign — that we can't help assigning — to the disaster that looms before us devalues morality itself and leaves us free to do whatever is militarily necessary to avoid the disaster, so long as what we do doesn't produce an even worse disaster. No great precision is required in calculations of this sort. Just as a jury in a capital case doesn't look for a 51 percent probability of guilt but for overwhelming certainty, so we can only be overwhelmed by supreme emergency. And, of course, we must always be skeptical about political leaders who are, so to speak, too easily overwhelmed, just as jurors must always be skeptical about those of their fellows who are too quick to place themselves "beyond a reasonable doubt."

But how can we be properly skeptical unless we have some precise understanding of what a supreme emergency is and how it differs from the daily emergencies of military life? I want to approach this question indirectly, by asking another. If we are permitted to respond immorally when a disaster threatens us, why can't an individual soldier respond immorally when a disaster threatens him? From the standpoint of the combat soldier, war is a rapid succession of supreme emergencies: his life is constantly at risk. But we are very reluctant to allow soldiers to save themselves by killing innocent and helpless people. Consider the standard case of soldiers holding prisoners behind enemy lines. I can't repeat here all the arguments that have been made about this much discussed and not at all hypothetical example. There is a range of conclusions, and considerable disagreement among commentators, but almost no one would say that the soldiers can kill their prisoners simply in order to reduce the danger to themselves.[8] Perhaps they can kill them if that is or seems to be absolutely necessary for the success of their mission, but once the mission has succeeded, they are commonly expected to bear some risk, even considerable risk, for the sake of their prisoners. And yet, what is at risk is all they have, life itself. So far as individuals are concerned, supreme emergency doesn't make a radical exception to rights normality. In war, as in domestic society, there are limits on what we can do in self-defense, even in extreme situations. A moral person will accept risk, will even accept death, rather than kill the innocent. But a moral president or prime minister or military commander will not accept the risk or the fact of communal death. Why not?

The first answer to this question has to do with the theory of representation. I can, morally and psychologically, accept risks for myself, but I can't, either morally or psychologically, accept risks for other people. If I possess political authority, I can impose risks, but I have only a limited right to do that (both the rights and the limits are implicit in the governmental contract). Soldiers, for example, are conscripted and then trained for risk-taking by the government in the name of the political community. But no government can put the life of the community itself and of all its members at risk, so long as there are actions available to it, even immoral actions, that would avoid or reduce the risk. It is for the sake of risk avoidance or risk reduction that governments are chosen. That is what political leaders are for; that is their first task. This argument, however, faces a deep difficulty. If individuals have no right to save themselves by killing the innocent, how can they commission their government to do this on their behalf? They can't pass on rights they don't possess, hence their political leaders can do no more on their behalf than they might do themselves. Leaders can act to reduce or avoid risks only within the limits of rights normality.

The argument from representation doesn't work unless we add to it an argument about the value of the community.[9] It isn't only individuals who are represented, but also the collective entity — religious, political, or cultural — that the individuals compose and from which they derive some portion of their character, practices, and beliefs. I don't want to say that the whole is greater than the sum of its parts, for I don't know how to sum the parts or set a value on the whole. A certain number of individuals can always be found — so it seems — who value the whole more than their own part; they are ready to risk their lives for their country. But it doesn't follow from this that they (or their leaders, acting on their behalf) are entitled to risk the lives of other people who don't even live in their country. There can't be any such entitlement. The risks imposed on the others are criminally imposed. How can the community permit or require criminal actions?

Edmund Burke's description of the political community as a contract between "those who are living, those who are dead, and those who are yet to be born" helps us to see what is at stake here.[10] The metaphor, I suppose, is inappropriate, since it is impossible to imagine the occasion on which such a contract could have been agreed to. But there is an important truth here nonetheless: we do try to carry on, and also to improve upon, a way of life handed down by our ancestors, and we do hope for recognizable descendants, carrying on and improving upon our own way of life. This commitment to continuity across generations is a very powerful feature of human life, and it is embodied in the community. When our community is threatened, not just in its present territorial extension or governmental structure or prestige or honor, but in what we might think of as its *ongoingness*, then we face a loss that is greater than any we can imagine, except for the destruction of humanity itself. We face moral as well as physical extinction, the end of a way of life as well as of a set of particular lives, the disappearance of people like us. And it is then that we may be driven to break through the moral limits that people like us normally attend to and respect.

By contrast, when we tell an individual soldier that he can't make the same break, we are telling him that he must risk death and even die within the moral limits so that his children and children's children can hope to live within them. It may be small comfort to a soldier facing death to know that people like himself will survive and continue to uphold the principles and practices he values (including the normal defense of rights, for if he didn't value that, there would be no issue here). But that knowledge is comfort enough to rule out any claim he might make to exempt himself from the moral prohibitions. Take that knowledge away, and the claim begins to seem plausible; and only then do we enter the terrible world of supreme emergency.

If the political community were nothing more than a neutral framework within which individuals pursued their own versions of the good life, as some liberal political philosophers suggest, the doctrine of supreme emergency would have no purchase.[11] It would indeed be a bad thing for individuals to lose the protection of such a framework, and they might be persuaded to accept some risk to their own lives in order to guard against that loss — though it's a hard question, first posed by Thomas Hobbes, the first theorist of the neutral framework, why anyone should die for a "community" whose substantive meaning only he can provide, and only so long as he is alive.[12] In any case, this kind of a person, facing this kind of a loss, can hardly drag other men and women (and children) into the war zone, from which he is likely to make his own escape as soon as he can. The license of supreme emergency can only be claimed by political leaders whose people have already risked everything and who know how much they have at risk.

The fact that a "communitarian" political theory helps to explain the meaning of supreme emergency might well be taken as an argument against communitarianism. For if we didn't value the community (however we conceive community: people, nation, country, religion, common culture) in this intense way, we might fight fewer wars and face fewer emergencies. Fewer emergencies, and none of them supreme, for in an international society composed of countries that were nothing more than neutral frameworks, or in an international society that was itself one big neutral framework, individuals pursuing their private projects might find many occasions for quarrels and even for fights but few for wars — they would have every reason to stop short of the kinds of risk that war involves. But this is only to say that life would be safer without emotional entanglements. The statement is obviously true but not very helpful.

Supreme emergency is a communitarian doctrine. But to say that is not to diminish the moral significance of the individual. Communities need, and can't always find, morally strong citizens, soldiers, and political and military leaders. And *morally* strong is very strong indeed, for what the community requires of individual citizens and soldiers is that they risk their lives, first for their compatriots and then for the innocent members of other countries. And what it requires of its leaders is that they impose risks and sometimes, in rare and terrible moments, take on the guilt of killing the innocent. We may doubt that moral strength is really required in this last instance; after all, many, perhaps most, of the political leaders who figure in the history books or in our own memories of twentieth-century history seem to have had no difficulty killing innocent people. They had no sense of the guilt involved; they were simply criminals. A morally strong leader is someone who understands why it is wrong to kill the innocent and refuses to do so, refuses again and again, until the heavens are about to fall. And then he becomes a moral criminal (like Albert Camus's "just assassin")[13] who knows that he can't do what he has to do — and finally does.

Provocation and paradox again. And yet this is not an idiosyncratic argument; I didn't make it up. It conforms to the professional ethic of the soldier as this has developed over the course of time, and also to the professional ethic of the police, firefighters, and merchant sailors, all of whom are required to risk their lives to protect the innocent. And it also conforms to the doctrine of "dirty hands," according to which political and military leaders may sometimes find themselves in situations where they cannot avoid acting immorally, even when that means deliberately killing the innocent.[14] The effect of the supreme-emergency argument should be to reinforce professional ethics and to provide an account of when it is permissible (or necessary) to get our hands dirty. The argument is essentially negative in character, as arguments have to be, I think, when they are focused on extreme cases, for dirty hands aren't permissible (or necessary) when anything less than the ongoingness of the community is at stake, or when the danger that we face is anything less than communal death. In most wars, the issue never arises; there are no supreme emergencies; the normal defense of rights holds unquestioned sway, even at the moment of defeat. In a war over this or that piece of territory, for example, we are not called upon to calculate how many innocent lives the territory is worth. If we are considering a strategy that involves deliberate murder (I leave aside questions about the side effects of legitimate military actions), the territory has to be deemed worthless, and innocence, as the normal defense of rights holds, beyond price.

Even in wars where the stakes are very high, they may not be so high at every moment in the course of the war as to bring the supreme-emergency argument into play. Each moment is a moment-in-itself; we make judgments again and again, not once for each war. My claim that the British bombing of German cities might have been defensible in 1940 and '41 extends no further than those years. The bulk of the bombing that actually took place is certainly not defensible, for it took place after it had become clear that Germany could not win the war. The triumph of Nazism was no longer an imminent danger. Nor was the continued bombing designed (as it might have been) to deter or defeat the Nazi war against the Jews. The Holocaust might have constituted a new supreme emergency, but it did not figure in the minds of the men who decided on bombing policy; they did not conceive themselves to be acting on behalf of the community of European Jewry.

The evil of Nazism suggests the positive form of the supreme-emergency argument. It is that sort of evil, uncommon even in the long history of human violence, that pushes us beyond rights normality. The more ordinary sorts of military defeat, political subjugation, the establishment of puppet regimes and satellite states — none of this qualifies as a similar "push," for in these cases we commonly expect the physical and moral survival of the defeated nation; we even look forward to its renewed resistance. Conventional conquerors, such as Alexander or Napoleon, leave behind more or less intact political and religious communities. It was the Nazi intention, at least in central and eastern Europe, not to do that; and even in the west, a long-term Nazi triumph would have brought a loss of value greater than men and women are morally obliged to bear. Only a prospect like that invites — and then only insofar as it also requires — an immoral response: we do what we must (every legitimate alternative having been exhausted). And if we can see clearly, with the help of such an example, when the normal defense of rights can be overridden, we can also see clearly why it can't be overridden short of that. For the overriding is also a loss of value, an action of exactly the sort that we anticipate from the other side and hope to avoid. In supreme emergencies, we imitate our worst enemies (as the bombing of Germany imitated the bombing of Coventry and the London blitz), and that is not something to which we can ever be reconciled.

It follows from this argument that supreme emergency is a condition from which we must seek an escape. Mostly, we will want to escape, for we will dread the dangers we face and abhor the immoral acts to which we are driven. But just as a "state of emergency" may be politically convenient for leaders who prefer to rule outside the law, so a state of supreme emergency may be morally convenient for leaders who wish to dispense with prohibitions and taboos. It is not always the case, of course, that emergencies are temporary in character; great dangers can persist over time. But we are morally bound to work against the persistence, to look for a way out, lest we be thought to view our dirty hands with less than abhorrence. The obvious example here is the cold war "balance of terror" generated by the deterrent policies of the United States and the Soviet Union. I suggested in *Just and Unjust Wars* that nuclear deterrence was commonly defended, and rightly defended, in terms that follow closely the lines of the supreme-emergency argument. Were terror unbalanced — so both sides believed — country and culture, people and way of life, would alike be at risk. And so we permitted ourselves to threaten the same terrorism that we feared: the destruction of cities, the killing of vast numbers of innocent men, women, and children. The threat was immoral, for it is wrong to threaten to do what it would be wrong to do; and though the threat is obviously a lesser wrong than the act, it can hardly be taken lightly when it is accompanied by massive preparation for the act.

We accepted the risk of nuclear war in order to avoid the risk, not of ordinary, but of totalitarian, subjugation. If that second risk were to recede (as it has), we would be bound to seek alternatives to deterrence in its cold-war form. In any case, we are bound to look for ways of reducing the risk — by pursuing détente, for example, or by signing arms-control and arms-reduction agreements, or by undertaking unilateral initiatives that address the fears and suspicions of the other side. We must resist the routinization of emergency, reminding ourselves again and again that the threats we force others to live with, and live with ourselves, are immoral threats. Over the years we became habituated, callous, hardened against the crimes we were pledged to commit. But it isn't incompatible with the pledge to think concretely about those crimes and about our own unwilling criminality — for it won't be unwilling unless we think about it. This is the essential feature of emergency ethics: that we recognize at the same time the evil we oppose and the evil we do, and that we set ourselves, so far as possible, against both.

I come back at the end to the communitarian foundation of emergency ethics. The strongest argument against supreme emergency is that it makes a fetish of the political community. Not, I want to stress, of the state: the state is nothing more than an instrument of the community, a particular structure for organizing collective action that can always be replaced by some other structure. The political community (the community of faith too) can't be similarly replaced. It consists of men, women, and children living in a certain way, and its replacement would require either the elimination of the people or the coercive transformation of their way of life. Neither of these actions is morally acceptable. But the reason for this unacceptability has nothing to do with fetishism. The political community is not magical, not mysterious, and not necessarily an "object of irrational reverence" (the dictionary definition of a fetish). It is a feature of our lived reality, a source of our identity and self-understanding. We can indeed make a fetish out of it, as countless nationalists and communalists have done; this is to engage in a collective version of self-worship, which is likely to have moral consequences of the same sort as the individual versions have. Egoists and communalists, who recognize no one's rights but their own, act badly on the smallest pretext, at the first hint of danger (perhaps also at the first hint of advantage) to themselves. A non-fetishized community, by contrast, sustains the discipline of its soldiers and the restraint of its leaders, who thus act badly only at the last minute and under absolute necessity.

Here is the final provocation and paradox: moral communities make great immoralities morally possible. But they do this only in the face of a far greater immorality, as in the example of a Nazi-like attack on the very existence of a particular community, and only at the moment when this attack is near success, and only insofar as the immoral response is the only way of holding off that success. We can recognize a moral community by its respect for that reiterated word "only." Supreme emergency is not in fact a permissive doctrine. It can be put to ideological and apologetic uses, but that is true of every moral argument, including the argument for individual rights. Properly understood, supreme emergency strengthens rights normality by guaranteeing its possession of the greater part, by far, of the moral world. That is its message to people like us: that it is (almost) the whole of our duty to uphold the rights of the innocent.

TERRORISM: A CRITIQUE OF EXCUSES
(1988)

No one these days advocates terrorism, not even those who regularly practice it. The practice is indefensible now that it has been recognized, like rape and murder, as an attack upon the innocent. In a sense, indeed, terrorism is worse than rape and murder commonly are, for in the latter cases the victim has been chosen for a purpose; he or she is the direct object of attack, and the attack has some reason, however twisted or ugly it may be. The victims of a terrorist attack are third parties, innocent bystanders; there is no special reason for attacking them; anyone else within a large class of (unrelated) people will do as well. The attack is directed indiscriminately against the entire class. Terrorists are like killers on a rampage, except that their rampage is not just expressive of rage or madness; the rage is purposeful and programmatic. It aims at a general vulnerability: Kill these people in order to terrify those. A relatively small number of dead victims makes for a very large number of living and frightened hostages.

This, then, is the peculiar evil of terrorism — not only the killing of innocent people but also the intrusion of fear into everyday life, the violation of private purposes, the insecurity of public spaces, the endless coerciveness of precaution. A crime wave might, I suppose, produce similar effects, but no one plans a crime wave; it is the work of a thousand individual decision-makers, each one independent of the others, brought together only by the invisible hand. Terrorism is the work of visible hands; it is an organizational project, a strategic choice, a conspiracy to murder and intimidate . . . you and me. No wonder the conspirators have difficulty defending, in public, the strategy they have chosen.

The moral difficulty is the same, obviously, when the conspiracy is directed not against you and me but against *them* — Protestants, say, not Catholics; Israelis, not Italians or Germans; blacks, not whites. These "limits" rarely hold for long; the logic of terrorism steadily expands the range of vulnerability. The more hostages they hold, the stronger the terrorists are. No one is safe once whole populations have been put at risk. Even if the risk were contained, however, the evil would be no different. So far as individual Protestants or Israelis or blacks are concerned, terrorism is random, degrading, and frightening. That is its hallmark, and that, again, is why it cannot be defended.

But when moral justification is ruled out, the way is opened for ideological excuse and apology. We live today in a political culture of excuses. This is far better than a political culture in which terrorism is openly defended and justified, for the excuse at least acknowledges the evil. But the improvement is precarious, hard won, and difficult to sustain. It is not the case, even in this better world, that terrorist organizations are without supporters. The support is indirect but by no means ineffective. It takes the form of apologetic descriptions and explanations, a litany of excuses that steadily undercuts our knowledge of the evil. Today that knowledge is insufficient unless it is supplemented and reinforced by a systematic critique of excuses. That is my purpose here. I take the principle for granted: that every act of terrorism is a wrongful act. The wrongfulness of the excuses, however, cannot be taken for granted; it has to be argued. The excuses themselves are familiar enough, the stuff of contemporary political debate. I shall state them in stereotypical form. There is no need to attribute them to this or that writer, publicist, or commentator; my readers can make their own attributions.[1]

The most common excuse for terrorism is that it is a last resort, chosen only when all else fails. The image is of people who have literally run out of options. One by one, they have tried every legitimate form of political and military action, exhausted every possibility, failed everywhere, until no alternative remains but the evil of terrorism. They must be terrorists or do nothing at all. The easy response is to insist that, given this description of their case, they should do nothing at all; they have indeed exhausted their possibilities. But this response simply reaffirms the principle, ignores the excuse; this response does not attend to the terrorists' desperation. Whatever the cause to which they are committed, we have to recognize that, given the commitment, the one thing they cannot do is "nothing at all."

But the case is badly described. It is not so easy to reach the "last resort." To get there, one must indeed try everything (which is a lot of things) and not just once, as if a political party might organize a single demonstration, fail to win immediate victory, and claim that it was now justified in moving on to murder. Politics is an art of repetition. Activists and citizens learn from experience, that is, by doing the same thing over and over again. It is by no means clear when they run out of options, but even under conditions of oppression and war, citizens have a good run short of that. The same argument applies to state officials who claim that they have tried "everything" and are now compelled to kill hostages or bomb peasant villages. Imagine such people called before a judicial tribunal and required to answer the question, What exactly did you try? Does anyone

believe that they could come up with a plausible list? "Last resort" has only a notional finality; the resort to terror is ideologically last, not last in an actual series of actions, just last for
the sake of the excuse. In fact, most state officials and movement
militants who recommend a policy of terrorism recommend it
as a first resort; they are for it from the beginning, although
they may not get their way at the beginning. If they are honest,
then, they must make other excuses and give up the pretense of
the last resort.

[Would terrorism be justified in a "supreme emergency" as
that condition is described in "Emergency Ethics" (Chapter 3)?
It might be, but only if the oppression to which the terrorists
claimed to be responding was genocidal in character. Against the
imminent threat of political and physical extinction, extreme
measures can be defended, assuming that they have some chance
of success. But this kind of a threat has not been present in any of
the recent cases of terrorist activity. Terrorism has not been a
means of avoiding disaster but of reaching for political success.]

The second excuse is designed for national liberation movements struggling against established and powerful states. Now
the claim is that nothing else is possible, that no other strategy is
available except terrorism. This is different from the first excuse
because it does not require would-be terrorists to run through all
the available options. Or, the second excuse requires terrorists to
run through all the options in their heads, not in the world;
notional finality is enough. Movement strategists consider their
options and conclude that they have no alternative to terrorism.
They think that they do not have the political strength to try
anything else, and thus they do not try anything else. Weakness is
their excuse.

But two very different kinds of weakness are commonly confused here: the weakness of the movement vis-à-vis the opposing state and the movement's weakness vis-à-vis its own people. This second kind of weakness, the inability of the movement to mobilize the nation, makes terrorism the "only" option because it effectively rules out all the others: nonviolent resistance, general strikes, mass demonstrations, unconventional warfare, and so on. These options are only rarely ruled out by the sheer power of the state, by the pervasiveness and intensity of oppression. Totalitarian states may be immune to nonviolent or guerrilla resistance, but all the evidence suggests that they are also immune to terrorism. Or, more exactly, in totalitarian states state terror dominates every other sort. Where terrorism is a possible strategy for the oppositional movement (in liberal and democratic states, most obviously), other strategies are also possible if the movement has some significant degree of popular support. In the absence of popular support, terrorism may indeed be the one available strategy, but it is hard to see how its evils can then be excused. For it is not weakness alone that makes the excuse, but the claim of the terrorists to represent the weak; and the particular form of weakness that makes terrorism the only option calls that claim into question.

One might avoid this difficulty with a stronger insistence on the actual effectiveness of terrorism. The third excuse is simply that terrorism works (and nothing else does); it achieves the ends of the oppressed even without their participation. "When the act accuses, the result excuses."[2] This is a consequentialist argument, and given a strict understanding of consequentialism, this argument amounts to a justification rather than an excuse. In practice, however, the argument is rarely pushed so far. More often, the argument begins with an acknowledgment of the terrorists' wrongdoing. Their hands are dirty, but we must make a kind of peace with them because they have acted effectively for the sake of people who could not act for themselves. But, in fact, have the terrorists' actions been effective? I doubt that terrorism has ever achieved national liberation—no nation that I know of owes its freedom to a campaign of random murder—although terrorism undoubtedly increases the power of the terrorists within the national liberation movement. Perhaps terrorism is also conducive to the survival and notoriety (the two go together) of the movement, which is now dominated by terrorists. But even if we were to grant some means-end relationship between terror and national liberation, the third excuse does not work unless it can meet the further requirements of a consequentialist argument. It must be possible to say that the desired end could not have been achieved through any other, less wrongful, means. The third excuse depends, then, on the success of the first or second, and neither of these look likely to be successful.

The fourth excuse avoids this crippling dependency. This excuse does not require the apologist to defend either of the improbable claims that terrorism is the last resort or that it is the only possible resort. The fourth excuse is simply that terrorism is the universal resort. All politics is (really) terrorism. The appearance of innocence and decency is always a piece of deception, more or less convincing in accordance with the relative power of the deceivers. The terrorist who does not bother with appearances is only doing openly what everyone else does secretly.

This argument has the same form as the maxim "All's fair in love and war." Love is always fraudulent, war is always brutal, and political action is always terrorist in character. Political action works (as Thomas Hobbes long ago argued) only by generating fear in innocent men and women. Terrorism is the politics of state officials and movement militants alike. This argument does not justify either the officials or the militants, but it does excuse them all. We hardly can be harsh with people who act the way everyone else acts. Only saints are likely to act differently, and sainthood in politics is supererogatory, a matter of grace, not obligation.

But this fourth excuse relies too heavily on our cynicism about political life, and cynicism only sometimes answers well to experience. In fact, legitimate states do not need to terrorize their citizens, and strongly based movements do not need to terrorize their opponents. Officials and militants who live, as it were, on the margins of legitimacy and strength sometimes choose terrorism and sometimes do not. Living in terror is not a universal experience. The world the terrorists create has its entrances and exits.

If we want to understand the choice of terror, the choice that forces the rest of us through the door, we have to imagine what in fact always occurs, although we often have no satisfactory record of the occurrence: A group of men and women, officials or militants, sits around a table and argues about whether or not to adopt a terrorist strategy. Later on, the litany of excuses obscures the argument. But at the time, around the table, it would have been no use for defenders of terrorism to say, "Everybody does it," because there they would be face to face with people proposing to do something else. Nor is it historically the case that the members of this last group, the opponents of terrorism, always lose the argument. They can win, however, and still not be able to prevent a terrorist campaign; the would-be terrorists (it does not take very many) can always split the movement and go their own way. Or, they can split the bureaucracy or the police or officer corps and act in the shadow of state power. Indeed, terrorism often has its origin in such splits. The first victims are the terrorists' former comrades or colleagues. What reason can we possibly have, then, for equating the two? If we value the politics of the men and women who oppose terrorism, we must reject the excuses of their murderers. Cynicism at such a time is unfair to the victims.

The fourth excuse can also take, often does take, a more restricted form. Oppression, rather than political rule more generally, is always terroristic in character, and thus, we must always excuse the opponents of oppression. When they choose terrorism, they are only reacting to someone else's previous choice, repaying in kind the treatment they have long received. Of course, their terrorism repeats the evil — innocent people are killed, who were never themselves oppressors — but repetition is not the same as initiation. The oppressors set the terms of the struggle. But if the struggle is fought on the oppressors' terms, then the oppressors are likely to win. Or, at least, oppression is likely to win, even if it takes on a new face. The whole point of a liberation movement or a popular mobilization is to change the terms. We have no reason to excuse the terrorism reactively adopted by opponents of oppression unless we are confident of the sincerity of their opposition, the seriousness of their commitment to a nonoppressive politics. But the choice of terrorism undermines that confidence.

We are often asked to distinguish the terrorism of the oppressed from the terrorism of the oppressors. What is it, however, that makes the difference? The message of the terrorist is the same in both cases: a denial of the peoplehood and humanity of the groups among whom he or she finds victims. Terrorism anticipates, when it does not actually enforce, political domination. Does it matter if one dominated group is replaced by another? Imagine a slave revolt whose protagonists dream only of enslaving in their turn the children of their masters. The dream is understandable, but the fervent desire of the children that the revolt be repressed is equally understandable. In neither case does understanding make for excuse — not, at least, after a politics of universal freedom has become possible. Nor does an understanding of oppression excuse the terrorism of the oppressed, once we have grasped the meaning of "liberation."

These are the four general excuses for terror, and each of them fails. They depend upon statements about the world that are false, historical arguments for which there is no evidence, moral claims that turn out to be hollow or dishonest. This is not to say that there might not be more particular excuses that have greater plausibility, extenuating circumstances in particular cases that we would feel compelled to recognize. As with murder, we can tell a story (like the story that Richard Wright tells in *Native Son*, for example) that might lead us, not to justify terrorism, but to excuse this or that individual terrorist. We can provide a personal history, a psychological study, of compassion destroyed by fear, moral reason by hatred and rage, social inhibition by unending violence — the product, an individual driven to kill or readily set on a killing course by his or her political leaders.[3] But the force of this story will not depend on any of the four general excuses, all of which grant what the storyteller will have to deny: that terrorism is the deliberate choice of rational men and women. Whether they conceive it to be one option among others or the only one available, they nevertheless argue and choose. Whether they are acting or reacting, they have made a decision. The human instruments they subsequently find to plant the bomb or shoot the gun may act under some psychological compulsion, but the men and women who choose terror as a policy act "freely." They could not act in any other way, or accept any other description of their action, and still pretend to be the leaders of the movement or the state. We ought never to excuse such leaders.

What follows from the critique of excuses? There is still a great deal of room for argument about the best way of responding to terrorism. Certainly, terrorists should be resisted, and it is not likely that a purely defensive resistance will ever be sufficient. In this sort of struggle, the offense is always ahead. The technology of terror is simple; the weapons are readily produced and easy to deliver. It is virtually impossible to protect people against random and indiscriminate attack. Thus, resistance will have to be supplemented by some combination of repression and retaliation. This is a dangerous business because repression and retaliation so often take terroristic forms and there are a host of apologists ready with excuses that sound remarkably like those of the terrorists themselves. It should be clear by now, however, that counterterrorism cannot be excused merely because it is reactive. Every new actor, terrorist or counterterrorist, claims to be reacting to someone else, standing in a circle and just passing the evil along. But the circle is ideological in character; in fact, every actor is a moral agent and makes an independent decision.

Therefore, repression and retaliation must not repeat the wrongs of terrorism, which is to say that repression and retaliation must be aimed systematically at the terrorists themselves, never at the people for whom the terrorists claim to be acting. That claim is in any case doubtful, even when it is honestly made. The people do not authorize the terrorists to act in their name. Only a tiny number actually participate in terrorist activities; they are far more likely to suffer than to benefit from the terrorist program. Even if they supported the program and hoped to benefit from it, however, they would still be immune from attack — exactly as civilians in time of war who support the war effort but are not themselves part of it are subject to the same immunity. Civilians may be put at risk by attacks on military targets, as by attacks on terrorist targets, but the risk must be kept to a minimum, even at some cost to the attackers. The refusal to make ordinary people into targets, whatever their nationality or even their politics, is the only way to say no to terrorism. Every act of repression and retaliation has to be measured by this standard.

But what if the "only way" to defeat the terrorists is to intimidate their actual or potential supporters? It is important to deny the premise of this question: that terrorism is a politics dependent on mass support. In fact, it is always the politics of an elite, whose members are dedicated and fanatical and more than ready to endure, or to watch others endure, the devastations of a counterterrorist campaign. Indeed, terrorists will welcome counterterrorism; it makes the terrorists' excuses more plausible and is sure to bring them, however many people are killed or wounded, however many are terrorized, the small number of recruits needed to sustain the terrorist activities.

Repression and retaliation are legitimate responses to terrorism only when they are constrained by the same moral principles that rule out terrorism itself. But there is an alternative response that seeks to avoid the violence that these two entail. The alternative is to address directly, ourselves, the oppression the terrorists claim to oppose. Oppression, they say, is the cause of terrorism. But that is merely one more excuse. The real cause of terrorism is the decision to launch a terrorist campaign, a decision made by that group of people sitting around a table whose deliberations I have already described. However, terrorists do exploit oppression, injustice, and human misery generally and look to these at least for their excuses. There can hardly be any doubt that oppression strengthens their hand. Is that a reason for us to come to the defense of the oppressed? It seems to me that we have our own reasons to do that, and do not need this one, or should not, to prod us into action. We might imitate those movement militants who argue against the adoption of a terrorist strategy — although not, as the terrorists say, because these militants are prepared to tolerate oppression. They already are opposed to oppression and now add to that opposition, perhaps for the same reasons, a refusal of terror. So should we have been opposed before, and we should now make the same addition.

But there is an argument, put with some insistence these days, that we should refuse to acknowledge any link at all between terrorism and oppression — as if any defense of oppressed men and women, once a terrorist campaign has been launched, would concede the effectiveness of the campaign. Or, at least, the defense would give terrorism the appearance of effectiveness and so increase the likelihood of terrorist campaigns in the future. Here we have the reverse side of the litany of excuses; we have turned over the record. First oppression is made into an excuse for terrorism, and then terrorism is made into an excuse for oppression. The first is the excuse of the far left; the second is the excuse of the neoconservative right.[4] I doubt that genuine conservatives would think it a good reason for defending the status quo that it is under terrorist attack; they would have independent reasons and would be prepared to defend the status quo against any attack. Similarly, those of us who think that the status quo urgently requires change have our own reasons for thinking so and need not be intimidated by terrorists or, for that matter, antiterrorists.

If one criticizes the first excuse, one should not neglect the second. But I need to state the second more precisely. It is not so much an excuse for oppression as an excuse for doing nothing (now) about oppression. The claim is that the campaign against terrorism has priority over every other political activity. If the people who take the lead in this campaign are the old oppressors, then we must make a kind of peace with them — temporarily, of course, until the terrorists have been beaten. This is a strategy that denies the possibility of a two-front war. So long as the men and women who pretend to lead the fight against oppression are terrorists, we can concede nothing to their demands. Nor can we oppose their opponents.

But why not? It is not likely in any case that terrorists would claim victory in the face of a serious effort to deal with the oppression of the people they claim to be defending. The effort would merely expose the hollowness of their claim, and the nearer it came to success, the more they would escalate their terrorism. They would still have to be defeated, for what they are after is not a solution to the problem but rather the power to impose their own solution. No decent end to the conflict in Ireland, say, or in Lebanon, or in the Middle East generally, is going to look like a victory for terrorism — if only because the different groups of terrorists are each committed, by the strategy they have adopted, to an indecent end.[5] By working for our own ends, we expose the indecency.

It is worth considering at greater length the link between oppression and terror. To pretend that there is no link at all is to ignore the historical record, but the record is more complex than any of the excuses acknowledge. The first thing to be read out of it, however, is simple enough: Oppression is not so much the cause of terrorism as terrorism is one of the primary means of oppression. This was true in ancient times, as Aristotle recognized, and it is still true today. Tyrants rule by terrorizing their subjects; unjust and illegitimate regimes are upheld through a combination of carefully aimed and random violence.[6] If this method works in the state, there is no reason to think that it will not work, or that it does not work, in the liberation movement. Wherever we see terrorism, we should look for tyranny and oppression. Authoritarian states, especially in the moment of their founding, need a terrorist apparatus — secret police with unlimited power, secret prisons into which citizens disappear, death squads in unmarked cars. Even democracies may use terror, not against their own citizens, but at the margins, in their colonies, for example, where colonizers also are likely to rule tyrannically. Oppression is sometimes maintained by a steady and discriminate pressure, sometimes by intermittent and random violence — what we might think of as terrorist melodrama — designed to render the subject population fearful and passive.

This latter policy, especially if it seems successful, invites imitation by opponents of the state. But terrorism does not spread only when it is imitated. If it can be invented by state officials, it can also be invented by movement militants. Neither one need take lessons from the other; the circle has no single or necessary starting point. Wherever it starts, terrorism in the movement is tyrannical and oppressive in exactly the same way as is terrorism in the state. The terrorists aim to rule, and murder is their method. They have their own internal police, death squads, disappearances. They begin by killing or intimidating those comrades who stand in their way, and they proceed to do the same, if they can, among the people they claim to represent. If terrorists are successful, they rule tyrannically, and their people bear, without consent, the costs of the terrorists' rule. (If the terrorists are only partly successful, the costs to the people may be even greater: What they have to bear now is a war between rival terrorist gangs.) But terrorists cannot win the ultimate victory they seek without challenging the established regime or colonial power and the people it claims to represent, and when terrorists do that, they themselves invite imitation. The regime may then respond with its own campaign of aimed and random violence. Terrorist tracks terrorist, each claiming the other as an excuse.

The same violence can also spread to countries where it has not yet been experienced; now terror is reproduced not through temporal succession but through ideological adaptation. State terrorists wage bloody wars against largely imaginary enemies: army colonels, say, hunting down the representatives of "international communism." Or movement terrorists wage bloody wars against enemies with whom, but for the ideology, they could readily negotiate and compromise: nationalist fanatics committed to a permanent irredentism. These wars, even if they are without precedents, are likely enough to become precedents, to start the circle of terror and counterterror, which is endlessly oppressive for the ordinary men and women whom the state calls its citizens and the movement its "people."

The only way to break out of the circle is to refuse to play the terrorist game. Terrorists in the state and the movement warn us, with equal vehemence, that any such refusal is a sign of softness and naiveté. The self-portrait of the terrorists is always the same. They are tough-minded and realistic; they know their enemies (or privately invent them for ideological purposes); and they are ready to do what must be done for victory. Why then do terrorists turn around and around in the same circle? It is true: Movement terrorists win support because they pretend to deal energetically and effectively with the brutality of the state. It also is true: State terrorists win support because they pretend to deal energetically and effectively with the brutality of the movement. Both feed on the fears of brutalized and oppressed people. But there is no way of overcoming brutality with terror. At most, the burden is shifted from these people to those; more likely, new burdens are added for everyone. Genuine liberation can come only through a politics that mobilizes the victims of brutality and takes careful aim at its agents, or by a politics that surrenders the hope of victory and domination and deliberately seeks a compromise settlement. In either case, once tyranny is repudiated, terrorism is no longer an option. For what lies behind all the excuses, of officials and militants alike, is the predilection for a tyrannical politics.

THE POLITICS OF RESCUE

(1994)

To intervene or not? — this should always be a hard question. Even in the case of a brutal civil war or a politically induced famine or the massacre of a local minority, the use of force in other people's countries should always generate hesitation and anxiety. So it does today among small groups of concerned people, some of whom end up supporting, some resisting, interventionist policies. But many governments and many more politicians seem increasingly inclined to find the question easy: the answer is *not!* Relatively small contingents of soldiers will be sent to help out in cases where it isn't expected that they will have to fight — thus the United States in Somalia, the Europeans in Bosnia, the French in Rwanda. The aim in all these countries (though we experimented briefly with something more in Mogadishu) is not to alter power relations on the ground, but only to ameliorate their consequences — to bring food and medical supplies to populations besieged and bombarded, for example, without interfering with the siege or bombardment.

This might be taken as a triumph for the old principle of nonintervention, except that the reasons on which the principle is based, which I will rehearse in a moment, do not appear to be the reasons that move governments and politicians today. They are not focused on the costs of intervention or, for that matter, of nonintervention to the men and women whose danger or suffering poses the question, but only on the costs to their own soldiers and to themselves, that is, to their political standing at home. No doubt, governments must think about such things: political leaders have to maintain their domestic support if they are to act effectively abroad. But they must also *act effectively abroad* when the occasion demands it, and they must be able to judge the urgency of the demand in the appropriate moral and political terms. The ideology of the cold war once provided a set of terms, not in fact always appropriate to the cases at hand, but capable of overriding domestic considerations. In the aftermath of the cold war, no comparable ideology has that capacity. The question, to intervene or not? gets answered every day, but with no sign that the judgments it requires are actually being made.

I am going to focus on the arguments for and against "humanitarian intervention," for this is what is at issue in the former Yugoslavia, the Caucasus, parts of Asia, much of Africa. Massacre, rape, ethnic cleansing, state terrorism, contemporary versions of "bastard feudalism," complete with ruthless warlords and lawless bands of armed men: these are the acts and occasions that invite us, or require us, to override the presumption against moving armies across borders and using force inside countries that have not threatened or attacked their neighbors. There is no external aggression to worry about, only domestic brutality, civil war, political tyranny, ethnic or religious persecution. When should the world's agents and powers (the United Nations, the European Community, the Pan American Alliance, the Organization of African Unity, the United States) merely watch and protest? When should they protest and then intervene?

The presumption against intervention is strong; we (on the left especially) have reasons for it, which derive from our opposition to imperial politics and our commitment to self-determination, even when the process of self-determination is something less than peaceful and democratic. Ever since Roman times, empires have expanded by intervening in civil wars, replacing "anarchy" with law and order, overthrowing supposedly noxious regimes. Conceivably, this expansion has saved lives, but only by creating in the process a "prison-house of nations," whose subsequent history is a long tale of prison revolts, brutally repressed. So it seems best that people who have lived together in the past and will have to do so in the future should be allowed to work out their difficulties without imperial assistance, among themselves. The resolution won't be stable unless it is locally grounded; there is little chance that it will be consensual unless it is locally produced.

Still, nonintervention is not an absolute moral rule: sometimes, what is going on locally cannot be tolerated. Hence the practice of "humanitarian intervention" — much abused, no doubt, but morally necessary whenever cruelty and suffering are extreme and no local forces seem capable of putting an end to them. Humanitarian interventions are not justified for the sake of democracy or free enterprise or economic justice or voluntary association or any other of the social practices and arrangements that we might hope for or even call for in other people's countries. Their aim is profoundly negative in character: to put a stop to actions that, to use an old-fashioned but accurate phrase, "shock the conscience" of humankind. There are some useful, and to my mind justified, contemporary examples: India in East Pakistan, Tanzania in Uganda, Vietnam in Cambodia. Interventions of this sort are probably best carried out by neighbors, as in these three cases, since neighbors will have some understanding of the local culture. They may also, however, have old scores to settle or old (or new) ambitions to dominate the neighborhood. If we had more trust in the effectiveness of the United Nations or the various regional associations, we could require international or at least multilateral endorsement, cooperation, and constraint. I will consider this possibility later on. It might be a way of controlling the economically or politically self-aggrandizing interventions of single states. For now, though, the agent-of-last-resort is anyone near enough and strong enough to stop what needs stopping.

But that's not always easy. On the standard view of humanitarian intervention (which I adopted when writing *Just and Unjust Wars* almost twenty years ago), the source of the inhumanity is conceived as somehow external and singular in character: a tyrant, a conqueror or usurper, or an alien power set over against a mass of victims. The intervention then has an aim that is simple as well as negative: remove the tyrant (Pol Pot, Idi Amin), set the people free (Bangladesh), and then get out. Rescue the people in trouble from their troublers, and let them get on with their lives. Help them, and then leave them to manage as best they can by themselves. The test of a genuinely humanitarian intervention, on this view, is that the intervening forces are quickly in and out. They do not intervene and then stay put for reasons of their own, as the Vietnamese did in Cambodia.

But what if the trouble is internal, the inhumanity locally and widely rooted, a matter of political culture, social structures, historical memories, ethnic fear, resentment, and hatred? Or what if the trouble follows from state failure, the collapse of any effective government, with results closer to Hobbes's than to Kropotkin's predictions—not quite a "war of all against all" but a widely dispersed, disorganized, and murderous war of some against some? No doubt, there are still identifiable evildoers, but now,

let's say, they have support at home, reserves, evildoers in waiting: what then? And what if there are overlapping sets of victims
and victimizers, like the Somalian clans and warlords or, perhaps,
the religious/ethnic/national groupings in Bosnia? In all these
cases, it may well happen that the quick departure of the intervening forces is followed immediately by the reappearance of the
conditions that led to intervention in the first place. Give up the
idea of an external and singular evil, and the "in and out" test is
very hard to apply.

We are extraordinarily dependent on the victim/victimizer,
good guys/bad guys model. I am not sure that any very forceful
intervention is politically possible without it. One of the reasons
for the weakness of the United Nations in Bosnia has been that
many of its representatives on the ground do not believe that the
model fits the situation they have to confront. They are not quite
apologists for the Serbs, who have (rightly) been condemned in
many United Nations resolutions, but they do not regard the
Serbs as wholly "bad guys" or as the only "bad guys" in the
former Yugoslavia. And that has made it difficult for them to
justify the measures that would be necessary to stop the killing
and the ethnic cleansing. Imagine that they took those measures,
as (in my view) they should have done: wouldn't they also have
been required to take collateral measures against the Croats and
Bosnian Moslems? In cases like this one, the politics of rescue is
certain to be complex and messy.

It is much easier to go into a place like Bosnia than to get out,
and the likely costs to the intervening forces and the local population are much higher than in the classic humanitarian interventions of the recent past. That is why American politicians and
military officers have insisted that there must be an exit strategy

before there can be an intervention. But this demand is effectively an argument against intervening at all. Exit strategies can rarely be designed in advance, and a public commitment to exit within such and such a time would give the hostile forces a strong incentive to lie low and wait. Better to stay home than to intervene in a way that is sure to fail.

Where the policies and practices that need to be stopped are widely supported, sustained by local structures and cultures, any potentially successful intervention is not going to meet the "in and out" test. It is likely to require a much more sustained challenge to conventional sovereignty: a long-term military presence, social reconstruction, what used to be called "political trusteeship" (since few of the locals — at least, the locals with power — can be trusted), and along the way, making all this possible, the large-scale and reiterated use of force. Is anyone ready for this? The question is especially hard for people on the left who are appalled by what happened or is happening in Bosnia, say, or Rwanda, but who have long argued, most of us, that the best thing to do with an army is to keep it at home. Even those who supported humanitarian interventions in the past have emphasized the moral necessity of a rapid withdrawal, leaving any ongoing use of force to indigenous soldiers.

Now this moral necessity seems to have become a practical, political necessity. Hence the general search for a quick fix, as in President Clinton's proposal (never very vigorously pursued) to "bomb the Serbs, arm the Bosnians." I would have supported both these policies, thinking that they might produce a local solution that, however bloody it turned out to be, could not be worse than what was happening anyway. But what if the quick fix failed, brought on an even more brutal civil war, with no end in sight?

Would we be ready then for a more direct and long-lasting military intervention — and if so, with what sort of an army? Under whose direction? With what weapons systems, what strategy and tactics, what willingness to take casualties and to impose them?

This last question is probably the crucial one in making intervention increasingly difficult and unlikely. It is very hard these days, in the Western democracies, to put soldiers at risk. But humanitarian interventions and peace-keeping operations are first of all military acts directed against people who are already using force, breaking the peace. They will be ineffective unless there is a willingness to accept the risks that naturally attach to military acts — to shed blood, to lose soldiers. In much of the world, bloodless intervention, peaceful peacekeeping is a contradiction in terms: if it were possible, it wouldn't be necessary. Insofar as it is necessary, we have to acknowledge the real status and function of the men and women whom we send to do the job. Soldiers are not like Peace Corps volunteers or Fulbright scholars or USIA musicians and lecturers — who should not, indeed, be sent overseas to dangerous places. Soldiers are destined for dangerous places, and they should know that (if they don't, they should be told).

This is not to say that soldiers should be sent recklessly into danger. But acknowledging their status and function poses the question that has to be answered before they are sent anywhere, at the moment their mission is being defined: is this a cause for which we are prepared to see American soldiers die? If this question gets an affirmative answer, then we cannot panic when the first soldier or the first significant number of soldiers, like the eighteen infantrymen in Somalia, are killed in a firefight. The

Europeans in Bosnia, it has to be said, didn't even wait to panic: they made it clear from the beginning that the soldiers they sent to open roads and transport supplies were not to be regarded as *soldiers* in any usual sense; these were grown-up Boy Scouts, doing good deeds. But this is a formula for failure. The soldiers who were not soldiers became, in effect, hostages of the Serbian forces that controlled the roads: subject to attack if anyone challenged that control. And the European governments became in turn the opponents of any such challenge.

Should we put soldiers at risk in faraway places when our own country is not under attack or threatened with attack (not Maine or Georgia or Oregon) and when national interests, narrowly understood, are not at stake? I am strongly inclined, sometimes, to give a positive answer to this question (whether volunteers or conscripts should bear these risks is too complicated to take up here). The reason is simple enough: all states have an interest in global stability and even in global humanity, and in the case of wealthy and powerful states like ours, this interest is seconded by obligation. No doubt, the "civilized" world is capable of living with grossly uncivilized behavior in places like East Timor, say— offstage and out of sight. But behavior of that kind, unchallenged, tends to spread, to be imitated or reiterated. Pay the moral price of silence and callousness, and you will soon have to pay the political price of turmoil and lawlessness nearer home.

I concede that these successive payments are not inevitable, but they come in sequence often enough. We see the sequence most clearly in Hannah Arendt's description of how European brutality in the colonies was eventually carried back to Europe itself. But the process can work in other ways too, as when terrorist regimes in the third world imitate one another (often with help from the first world), and waves of desperate refugees flee into countries where powerful political forces, not yet ascendent, want only to drive them back. For how long will decency survive *here*, if there is no decency *there?* Now obligation is seconded by interest.

As I have already acknowledged, interest and obligation together have often provided an ideology for imperial expansion or cold war advance. So it's the political right that has defended both, while the left has acquired the habit of criticism and rejection. But in this post-imperial and post–cold war age, these positions are likely to be reversed or, at least, confused. Many people on the right see no point in intervention today when there is no material or, for that matter, ideological advantage to be gained. "What's Bosnia to them or they to Bosnia/that they should weep for her?" And a small but growing number of people on the left now favor intervening, here or there, driven by an internationalist ethic. They are right to feel driven. Internationalism has always been understood to require support for, and even participation in, popular struggles anywhere in the world. But that meant: we have to wait for the popular struggles. Liberation should always be a local initiative. In the face of human disaster, however, internationalism has a more urgent meaning. It's not possible to wait; anyone who can take the initiative should do so. Active opposition to massacre and massive deportation is morally necessary; its risks must be accepted.

Even the risk of a blocked exit and a long stay. These days, for reasons we should probably celebrate, countries in trouble are no longer viewed as imperial opportunities. Instead, the metaphors are ominous: they are "bogs" and "quagmires." Intervening armies won't be defeated in these sticky settings, but they will suffer a slow attrition — and show no quick or obvious benefits. How did the old empires ever get soldiers to go to such places, to sit in beleaguered encampments, to fight an endless round of small, wearying, unrecorded battles? Today, when every death is televised, democratic citizens (the soldiers themselves or their parents) are unlikely to support or endure interventions of this kind. And yet, sometimes, they ought to be supported and endured. Consider: if some powerful state or regional alliance had rushed troops into Rwanda when the massacres first began or as soon as their scope was apparent, the massacre, the exodus, and the cholera plague might have been avoided. But the troops would still be there, probably, and no one would know what hadn't happened.

Two forms of long-lasting intervention, both associated in the past with imperial politics, now warrant reconsideration. The first is a kind of trusteeship, where the intervening power actually rules the country it has "rescued," acting in trust for the inhabitants, seeking to establish a stable and more or less consensual politics. The second is a kind of protectorate, where the intervention brings some local group or coalition of groups to power and is then sustained only defensively, to ensure that there is no return of the defeated regime or the old lawlessness and that minority rights are respected. Rwanda might have been a candidate for trusteeship; Bosnia for a protectorate.

These are arrangements that are hard to recommend and that would, no doubt, be hard to justify in today's political climate. The lives they saved would be speculative and statistical, not actual lives; only disasters that *might have* occurred (but how can we be sure?) would be avoided. This is rescue-in-advance, and it will be resisted by those local elites who believe that the need for rescue will never arise if they are allowed to take charge — or who are prepared to take charge at any cost. The very idea of a "failed state" will seem patronizing and arrogant to a group like, say, the Rwandan Patriotic Front, which hasn't yet had a chance to succeed. Nor is the history of trusteeships and protectorates particularly encouraging: the contemporary horror of the Sudanese civil war, for example, is no reason to forget the oppressiveness of the old "Anglo-Egyptian Sudan." Nonetheless, given what is now going on in Southeast Europe and Central Africa, morally serious people have to think again about the human costs and benefits of what we might call "standing interventions." Haiti today [October 1994] might provide a test case, since the U.S.-led, multinational force serves as the protector of the restored Aristide government — and that role is likely to be an extended one.

Who will, who should, do the "standing" and pay the price of the possible but often invisible victories? This is no doubt the hardest question, but it isn't, curiously, the one that has attracted the most attention. The public debate has had a different focus — as if there were (as perhaps there once were) a large number of states eager to intervene. So the question is: who can authorize and constrain these interventions, set the ground rules and the time frame, worry about their strategies and tactics? The standard answer on the left, and probably more widely, is that the best authority is international, multilateral — the U.N. is the obvious example. Behind this preference is an argument something like Rousseau's argument for the general will: in the course of a democratic decision procedure, Rousseau claimed, the particular interests of the different parties will cancel each other out, leaving a general interest untainted by particularity. As with individuals in domestic society, so with states in international society: if all of them are consulted, each will veto the self-aggrandizing proposals of the others.

But this isn't a wholly attractive idea, for its result is very likely to be stalemate and inaction, which cannot always be the general will of international society. It is also possible, of course, that some coalition of states, cooperating for the sake of shared (particular) interests, will have its way; or that stalemate will free the U.N.'s bureaucracy to pursue a program of its own. Multilateralism is no guarantee of anything. It may still be better than the unilateral initiative of a single powerful state — though in the examples with which I began, India, Vietnam, and Tanzania, local powers did not do entirely badly; none of their interventions, with the possible exception of the last, would have been authorized by the U.N. In practice, we should probably look for some concurrence of multilateral authorization and unilateral initiative — the first for the sake of moral legitimacy, the second for the sake of political effectiveness — but it's the initiative that is essential.

Can we assume that there are states ready to take the initiative and sustain it? In Somalia, the United States made the undertaking but was unprepared for the long haul. Bosnia provides a classic example of a serial rejection of the undertaking: everyone deplored the war and the ethnic cleansing; no one was prepared to stop them — and no one is prepared now to reverse their effects. Similarly, the African states and the Western powers stood by and watched the Rwandan massacres. (Remember the biblical injunction: "Do not stand idly by the blood of thy neighbor." The Rwandans, it turned out, had no local or global neighbors until they were dying by the thousands on foreign soil and on television.) It seems futile to say what is also obvious: that some states should be prepared to intervene in some cases. It is probably equally futile to name the states and the cases, though that is what I mean to do, on the principle that even futility is improved when it is made less abstract. The European Community or, at least, the French and British together (the Germans were disqualified by their aggression in World War II) ought to have intervened early on in Bosnia. The Organization of African Unity, with the financial help of Europeans and Americans, should have intervened early on in Rwanda. (I concede that the Nigerian-led intervention in Liberia is not an entirely happy precedent, though it has probably slowed the killing.) The United States should have intervened in Haiti months before it did, though the probably necessary protectorate would best have been undertaken by a coalition of Central American and Caribbean states. It is harder to say who should have stopped the killing in southern Sudan or East Timor: there isn't always an obvious candidate or a clear responsibility. It is also hard to say how responsibility passes on, when the obvious candidates refuse its burdens. Should the United States, as the world's only or greatest "great power" be nominated agent-of-last-resort? With the transportation technology at our command, we are probably near enough, and we are certainly strong enough, to stop what needs stopping in most of the cases I have been discussing (though not in all of them at once).

But no one really wants the United States to become the world's policeman, even of-last-resort, as we would quickly see were we to undertake the role. Morally and politically, a division of labor is better, and the best use of American power will often be to press other countries to do their share of the work. Still, we will, and we should be, more widely involved than other countries with fewer resources. Sometimes, the United States should take the initiative; sometimes we should help pay for and even add soldiers to an intervention initiated by somebody else. In many cases, nothing at all will be done unless we are prepared to play one or the other of these parts — either the political lead or a combination of financial backer and supporting player. Old and well-earned suspicions of American power must give way now to a wary recognition of its necessity. (A friend comments: you would stress the wariness more if there were a Republican president. Probably so.)

Many people on the left will long for a time when this necessary American role is made unnecessary by the creation of an international military force. But this time, though it will obviously come before the much heralded leap from the realm of necessity to the realm of freedom, is still a long way off. Nor would a U.N. army with its own officers, capable of acting independently in the field, always find itself in the right fields (that is, the killing fields). Its presence or absence would depend on decisions of a Security Council likely to be as divided and uncertain as it is today, still subject to great-power veto and severe budgetary constraints. The useful role played by the U.N. in Cambodia (organizing and supervising elections) suggests the importance of strengthening its hand. But it wasn't the U.N. that overthrew Pol Pot and stopped the Khmer Rouge massacres. And so long as we can't be sure of its ability and readiness to do that, we will have to look for and live with unilateral interventions. It is a good thing, again, when these are undertaken by local powers like Vietnam; most often, however, they will depend on global powers like the United States and (we can hope) the European Community.

Despite all that I have said so far, I don't mean to abandon the principle of nonintervention — only to honor its exceptions. It is true that right now there are a lot of exceptions. One reads the newspaper these days shaking. The vast numbers of murdered people; the men, women, and children dying of disease and famine willfully caused or easily preventable; the masses of desperate refugees — none of these are served by reciting high-minded principles. Yes, the norm is not to intervene in other people's countries; the norm is self-determination. But not for *these* people, the victims of tyranny, ideological zeal, ethnic hatred, who are not determining anything for themselves, who urgently need help from outside. And it isn't enough to wait until the tyrants, the zealots, and the bigots have done their filthy work and then rush food and medicine to the ragged survivors. Whenever the filthy work can be stopped, it should be stopped. And if not by us, the supposedly decent people of this world, then by whom?

PART TWO
cases

Political theories are tested by events in the political world. We ask whether the theory illuminates the events. Does it bring the right issues into relief? Is it helpful in shaping, justifying, and explaining our moral responses and judgments?

Consider the war in the Persian Gulf as a test case. Conscripted into service, how well did the theory of just war serve? Curiously, some critics of the war, particularly religious critics (some Catholic bishops, the leaders of the World Council of Churches), tried simultaneously to use and discard the theory. They talked about justice because they wanted to say that the war was unjust, and they discarded much of the theory of justice because they were afraid (or, better, acutely aware) that, in standard just war terms, it wasn't. They commonly ended up with an argument that seems to me both dangerous and wrong: that no war in the modern world can possibly be just. The theory for them has lost its capacity to make distinctions. Given the resources of a modern army, given the availability of weapons of mass destruction, the old categories can't do any serious work. We are left with a theory of justice that is obsolete and a practice of war that is obscene.

It is certainly possible to reinterpret or reconstruct just war theory so that no war could possibly be justified. It is important to stress, however, that "no war" here means *no war past or present.* The most massively destructive form of warfare is also one of the oldest: the siege of a city, in which the civilian population is the avowed target and no effort is made to single out soldiers and military bases for attack — one of the classic requirements of justice in war. Those opponents of the Gulf War who advocated a prolonged blockade of Iraq seem not to have realized that what they were advocating was a radically indiscriminate act of war, with predictably harsh consequences. Just war theory as I understand it would require that food and medical supplies be let through — but in that case it is unlikely that the blockade would serve its purpose. In any case, we have no reason to think that judgments of this sort are any more difficult now than they were hundreds or thousands of years ago. There never was a golden age of warfare when just war categories were easy to apply and therefore regularly applied. If anything, modern technology makes it possible to fight with greater discrimination now than in the past, if there is a political will to do so.

Nonetheless, it is possible to construe the theory so that discrimination between military and civilian targets becomes irrelevant. And then, as we will see, another distinction is also lost: between just war theory and pacifism. Some of the bishops, though still formally committed to the just war, seem to me to have moved in this direction. The move involves a new stress upon two maxims of the theory: first, that war must be a "last resort," and second, that its anticipated costs to soldiers and civilians alike must not be disproportionate to (greater than) the value of its ends. I do not think that either maxim helps us much in making the moral distinctions that we need to make. And the Gulf War provides a useful illustration of the inadequacy of the two.

I will begin with the sequence of events. Iraq invaded Kuwait in early August 1990; Kuwaiti resistance was brief and ineffective, and the country was occupied in a matter of days. That was the beginning, and might have been the end, of the war. There ensued a brief flurry of diplomatic activity, against a background of American mobilization and the arrival of U.S. troops in Saudi Arabia. The diplomacy produced an economic blockade of Iraq, sanctioned by the United Nations and militarily enforced by a coalition of states led and dominated by the United States. Though the blockade required very little military enforcement, it was technically and practically an act of war. But the common perception during those months (August 1990–January 1991) was that the Gulf was at peace, while the coalition tried to reverse the Iraqi aggression without violence and debated, in slow motion and cold blood, whether or not to begin the war. It was in the context of this debate that the question of "last resort" was posed.

Had the Kuwaiti army, against all the odds, succeeded in holding off the invaders for a few weeks or months, the question would never have arisen. War would have been the first resort of the Kuwaitis, acceptably so given the immediacy and violence of the invasion, and any allied or friendly state could legitimately have joined in their defense. The failure of the resistance opened a kind of temporal and moral hiatus during which it was possible to seek alternative resolutions of the conflict. The blockade was merely one of many alternatives, which included United Nations condemnation of Iraq, its diplomatic and political isolation, various degrees of economic sanction, and a negotiated settlement involving small or large concessions to the aggressor. The actual blockade might have taken different forms, adapted to different ends; the coalition might, for example, have aimed at the containment rather than the reversal of Iraqi aggression.

I assume that it was morally obligatory to canvass these possibilities and to weigh their likely consequences. But it is hard to see how it could have been obligatory to adopt one of them, or a sequence of them, simply so that war would be a "last resort." If the allies, weighing the consequences of the alternatives, one of which was the continued occupation of Kuwait, had decided on an early (September, say) ultimatum — withdraw or face a counterattack — the decision would not have been unjust. They would have had to allow a decent interval for the withdrawal to be considered and its modalities negotiated, and we would want some assurance that they had good reasons to think that other strategies would not work or would work only at great cost to the people of Kuwait. Given the interval and the reasons, the doctrine of "last resort" doesn't seem to play any important role here.

Taken literally, which is exactly the way many people took it during the months of the blockade, "last resort" would make war morally impossible. For we can never reach lastness, or we can never know that we have reached it. There is always something else to do: another diplomatic note, another United Nations resolution, another meeting. Once something like a blockade is in place, it is always possible to wait a little longer and hope for the success of (what looks like but isn't quite) nonviolence. Assuming, however, that war was justified in the first instance, at the moment of the invasion, then it is justifiable at *any* subsequent point when its costs and benefits seem on balance better than those of the available alternatives.

But sending troops into battle commonly brings with it so many unanticipated costs that it has come to represent a moral threshold: political leaders must cross this threshold only with great reluctance and trepidation. This is the truth contained in the "last resort" maxim. If there are potentially effective ways of avoiding actual fighting while still confronting the aggressor, they should be tried. In the hiatus months of the Gulf crisis, it seems to me that they were tried. The combination of economic blockade, military threat, and diplomatic deadline was a strategy plausibly designed to bring about an Iraqi withdrawal. Politics and war commonly work on timetables of this sort. Our blockade of Iraq was not a conventional siege, to be maintained until mass starvation forced Saddam Hussein's surrender. We were committed and, as I have already said, should have been committed to let food and medical supplies through before people started dying in the streets — though many people would have died anyway from the longer-term effects of malnutrition and disease. The blockade was aimed above all at Iraq's military-industrial capacity. But Saddam could have let this capacity run down over a period of months or even years, so long as he was sure that he wouldn't be attacked. Hence, the blockade's effectiveness depended on a credible threat to fight, and this threat, once it was mounted, could not be sustained indefinitely. At some point, the Iraqis had to yield or the coalition had to fight. If they didn't yield and it didn't fight, the victory would have been theirs: aggression triumphant. Most competent observers, applying this or that version of rational decision theory, expected Iraq to yield before the January 15 deadline. When that did not happen, war was, though not a "last," surely a legitimate resort.

But at this point the proportionality maxim is brought into play, and it is argued that war can never be legitimate under modern conditions because its costs will always be greater than its benefits. Certainly, we want political and military leaders to worry about costs and benefits. But they have to *worry;* they can't calculate, for the values at stake are not commensurate — at least they can't be expressed or compared mathematically, as the idea of proportion suggests. How do we measure the value of a country's independence against the value of the lives that might be lost in defending it? How do we figure in the value of defeating an aggressive regime (the invasion of Kuwait was not the first, nor was it likely to be the last, of Iraq's aggressions) or the value of deterring other, similar regimes? All values of this latter sort are likely to lose out to the body count, since it is only bodies that can be counted. And then it is impossible to fight any wars except those that promise to be bloodless, and not only on one side. This last is an entirely respectable position — pacifism, not just war — but anyone holding it will have to recognize and accept the non-pacific results of trying to accommodate states like Saddam Hussein's Iraq.

At the same time, no sane political leader would choose a war that brought millions or even hundreds of thousands of deaths, or that threatened the world with nuclear destruction, for the sake of Kuwaiti independence. This is the truth in the proportionality maxim. But it is a gross truth, and while it will do some work in cases like the Soviet Union's 1968 invasion of Czechoslovakia (no one proposed that the United States mobilize for a military response), it isn't going to make for useful discriminations in the greater number of cases. Most of the time, we can make only short-term predictions, and we have no way that even mimics mathematics of comparing the costs of fighting to the costs of not fighting, since one set of costs is necessarily speculative, while the other comes in, as it were, over an indeterminate time span. If we simply insist in advance that, given the weapons currently available, fighting is sure to produce catastrophic losses, the proportionality maxim would indeed rule out war in this and every other case: but this proposition is false.

We have to ask instead which particular weapons are likely to be used, how they will be used, and for what ends. About all these matters, just war theory has a great deal to say, and what it has to say is importantly restrictive. When it comes to resisting aggression, by contrast, the theory is at least permissive, sometimes imperative. Aggression is not only a crime against the formal rules of international society; it is also, more importantly, an assault upon a people, a threat to their common life and even their physical survival. That is why particular acts of aggression, like the Iraqi invasion, *ought to be resisted*—not necessarily by military means but by some means. Though military means may be ruled out in practice in this or that case (because they are unlikely to be effective, or because they are frighteningly dangerous), they are never ruled out in principle. It is our abhorrence of aggression that is authoritative here, while the maxims of "last resort" and proportionality play only marginal and uncertain roles.

Just wars are limited wars; their conduct is governed by a set of rules designed to bar, so far as possible, the use of violence and coercion against noncombatant populations. The "government" of these rules, since it is not backed up by police power or authoritative courts, is to a large degree ineffective — but not entirely so. And even if the rules fail to shape the conduct of *this* war, they often succeed in shaping public judgments of conduct and so, perhaps, the training, commitment, and future conduct of soldiers. If war is an extension of politics, then military culture is an extension of political culture. Debate and criticism play an important, even if not a determinative, role in fixing the content of both these cultures.

Two forms of limit are crucial here, and both figured largely in the political defense, and then in the critique, of the Gulf War. The first has to do with the ends of war, the purposes for which it is fought. Just war theory, as it is usually understood, looks to the restoration of the status quo ante — the way things were, that is, before the aggression took place — with only one additional proviso: that the threat posed by the aggressor state in the weeks or months before its attack should not be included in this "restoration." Hence war aims legitimately reach to the destruction or to the defeat, demobilization, and (partial) disarming of the aggressor's armed forces. Except in extreme cases, like that of Nazi Germany, they don't legitimately reach to the transformation of the internal politics of the aggressor state or the replacement of its regime. For ends of this latter sort would require a prolonged occupation and massive coercion of civilians. More than this: they would require a usurpation of sovereignty, which is exactly what we condemn when we condemn aggression.

In the Iraqi case, the acceptance of this limit by the coalition opened the way, after the cease-fire, for a bloody civil war, whose civilian casualties may well exceed those of the war itself. The proportionality maxim would probably have dictated a quick and militarily inexpensive march on Baghdad. Limited wars are governed instead by the doctrine of nonintervention, which holds that changes of regime must be the work of the men and women who live under the regime — who also bear the costs of the change and the risks of failure. Nonintervention gives way to proportionality only in cases of massacre or of politically induced famine and epidemic, when the costs are unbearable. Then we are justified in acting or, more strongly, we ought to act (like the Vietnamese in Pol Pot's Cambodia, or the Tanzanians in Idi

Amin's Uganda, or the Indians in what was then East Pakistan) without regard to the idea of sovereignty. It will seem hard to say, first, that we should not have intervened and made sure that the "right" side won the Iraqi civil war, and, second, that we should have intervened, much more quickly than we did, to rescue the victims of defeat. But the history of political, as distinct from humanitarian, interventions suggests that there are good reasons to make this distinction.

The same restorationist argument applies, more obviously, to the victim state, which is no more likely than the aggressor to be a bastion of sweetness and light (think of Haile Selassie's Ethiopian empire invaded by Italian fascists). Kuwait's regime was on balance superior to that of Iraq, but there are not many people in the world who would have rallied to its defense, even in print, had it been faced with a palace coup; a popular uprising would have been greeted almost everywhere with enthusiasm. And yet the purpose of the war was nothing more or less than the restoration of this regime, the semifeudal despotism of the al-Sabah family. What happened after that was (and is) the business of the Kuwaitis themselves, free from the coercion of foreign armies. They are not free, of course, from diplomatic pressure, or from human rights surveillance and agitation.

But the reversal of the aggression and the destruction of Iraqi military power were not the only goals of the coalition — or, at least, not the only goals of the United States in its role as organizer and leader of the coalition. Our government aimed also at a "new world order" in which its leading role, presumably, would be maintained. It was a common criticism of the war that the United States had "imperialist" motives: world order masked a desire for influence and power in the Gulf, for a strategic presence and control over the flow of oil. I assume that motives of this sort played an important part in American decision-making: even just wars have political as well as moral reasons — and will have, I expect, until the messianic age when justice will be done for its own sake. An absolutely singular motivation, a pure will, is a political illusion. The case is similar in domestic society, where we take it for granted that parties and movements fighting for civil rights or welfare reform do so because their members have certain values *and also* because they have certain ambitions — for power and office, say. Since they are not killing other people, this is easier to accept. But mixed motives are normal also in international politics, and they are morally troubling in wartime only if they make for the expansion or prolongation of the fighting beyond its justifiable limits or if they distort the conduct of the war.

It is entirely possible, then, to support a war within its justifiable limits and to oppose the added reasons this or that government has for fighting it. One could call for the defeat of Iraqi aggression and criticize at the same time the likely character of the "new world order." What is most important, however, is to insist that, new order or no, the war remain a limited war.

The second limit has to do with conduct — the everyday engagement of forces. The governing principle here is simply that every effort be made to protect civilian life from both direct attack and "collateral damage." How this principle fared in the Gulf War is best discussed in the context of the air campaign against Iraq, since war on the ground in desert environments tends to approach, effortlessly, as it were, the just war paradigm of a combat between combatants (there is still the question, though, of when and how such a combat should be brought to a halt). The coalition's military response to Iraq's invasion of Kuwait began with an air attack, and the war was fought almost exclusively with planes and missiles for some five weeks. The air war was described by American officers in press conferences and briefings in a language that combined technological jargon and just war theory. It was, we were told, a campaign directed with unprecedented precision solely at military targets. The bombs were "smart" and the pilots morally sensitive.

This effort to limit civilian casualties was embodied in clear-cut orders. Pilots were instructed to return to base with their bombs and missiles intact whenever they were unable to get a clear "fix" on their assigned targets. They were not to drop their bombs in the general vicinity of the targets; nor were they to aim freely at "targets of opportunity" (except in specified battle zones). In their bombing runs, they were to accept risks for themselves in order to reduce the risk of causing "collateral damage" to civilians. So we were told, and so, presumably, the pilots were told. The first studies of the bombing, after the war, suggest that those orders were often not followed — that bombs were commonly dropped from altitudes much too high for anything like confident aiming. But the policy, if it was the actual policy, was the right one. And it does appear that direct civilian casualties were kept fairly low: in this sense, at least, the air war was unprecedented.

The case is rather different if we look not at aiming policy but at the designated targets of that policy. The coalition decided (or the U.S. commanders decided) that the economic infrastructure of Iraqi society was — all of it — a legitimate military target: communication and transportation systems, electric power grids, government buildings of every sort, water pumping stations and purification plants. There was nothing unprecedented here; strategic bombing in World War II had a similar focus, though I don't believe that there was a systematic effort to deprive the German or Japanese people of clean water; perhaps this wasn't technically feasible in the 1940s. Selected infrastructural targets are easy enough to justify: bridges over which supplies are carried to the army in the field provide an obvious example. But power and water—water most clearly—are very much like food: they are necessary to the survival and everyday activity of soldiers, but they are equally necessary to everyone else. An attack here is an attack on civilian society. In this case, it is the military effects, if any, that are "collateral." The direct effect of the destruction of water purification plants, for example, was to impose upon civilians in urban areas (and Iraq is a highly urbanized society) the risks of disease in epidemic proportions.

Attacks of this sort suggest a war aim beyond the legitimate aim of "restoration plus"—the liberation of Kuwait and the defeat and reduction of Iraqi military power. The added, though never acknowledged, aim was presumably the overthrow of the Baathist regime, which was to be proven incapable not only of defending its foreign conquest but also of protecting its own people. But the aim is unjust and so is the means.

Indeed, even if we were justified in overthrowing the regime, we would have been barred from this cruel strategy of indirection—shattering Iraqi society so as to generate a desperate rebellion by its members. It would have been better to march on Baghdad. An exiled Iraqi dissident, writing just after the war, argued that since we had shattered Iraqi society, we were now bound to march on Baghdad and install a democratic government capable of organizing its reconstruction. I don't doubt that obligations of a significant sort can be incurred through wrongful actions in war. The difficulty with this particular example is the terrible presumption of the enterprise. Success was improbable anyway, and the likely human costs high.

There are other aspects of the conduct of the war that invite criticism and have received it — most importantly, the use of a frightening new weapon, the fuel air explosive, against Iraqi soldiers, and the air attacks, in the last days of the fighting, on what appears to have been not only an army in retreat but a routed and disorganized army in retreat. Just war theory as I understand it does not readily cover cases of this sort, where it is only soldiers who are under attack. Soldiers running away, unlike soldiers trying to surrender, are usually said to be legitimate targets: they may hope to fight another day. In this case, the Iraqi soldiers who succeeded in running away did fight another day — against rebellious fellow citizens. Here is yet another hard question for theorists of proportionality: should we have slaughtered retreating Iraqi soldiers in order to prevent the possible slaughter of Iraqi rebels? Standard just war arguments would probably come down against bombing the chaotic flight from Kuwait, precisely because the retreating army posed no threat *except* to its own people.

But this last point doesn't quite reach to our uneasiness with the spectacle of those last hours of the war, or to our relief when President Bush — too soon, some of his generals thought — called a halt to the killing. Justice is not the whole of morality. One may object to killing in war, even in just war, whenever it gets too easy. A "turkey shoot" is not a combat between combatants. When the world divides radically into those who bomb and those who are bombed, it becomes morally problematic, even if the bombing in this or that instance is justifiable.

It is still possible to defend some acts of war and unequivocally to condemn others. Nor can political and military leaders escape accountability by claiming that the acts that ought to be condemned were somehow entailed by the war itself and inevitable as soon as the fighting began. In fact, they required a distinct and independent decision by military strategists sitting around a table and arguing about what should be done — and then they required a further decision by politicians sitting around another table and arguing about the strategists' recommendations. It is easy enough to imagine the Gulf War without the attack on infrastructural targets. One might say that the point of just war theory is to make such imaginings obligatory.

seven

KOSOVO
(1999)

At this writing, the NATO bombing of Yugoslavia continues, and the Serbian destruction of Kosovar society also continues. Yes, the Serbian campaign must have been planned before the bombing began; the logistics of moving forty thousand soldiers are immensely complex. In some parts of Kosovo the harsh realities of ethnic cleansing were already visible before the decision to hit the Serbs with missiles and smart bombs was made. And given the Serbian record in Bosnia, and the mobilization of soldiers on the borders of Kosovo, and the refugees already on the move, military intervention seems to me entirely justified, even obligatory. But the brutal emptying of Kosovo in the weeks since is still in some sense a response to NATO's air campaign, and the speed with which it has been carried out is obviously a response — an effort to create facts on the ground before (as Milosevic apparently believes) the bombing stops and negotiations resume. Ethnic cleansing is perfectly consistent with the air campaign, and is partly its consequence.

I don't know what the expectations of NATO commanders were last March; ordinary citizens in the United States and Europe were certainly led to expect that the bombing would solve the problem fairly quickly. Once again, our faith in airpower is revealed as a kind of idolatry — we glorify the power of our own inventions. The truth remains, however, what it was before the inventions: soldiers with guns, going from house to house in a mountain village, can't be stopped by smart bombs. They can only be stopped by soldiers with guns.

But the countries involved in the NATO intervention are committed, for now at least, not to send in soldiers with guns. The promise wasn't made to Milosevic, obviously, but to the citizens of all the NATO countries: we won't send your children into battle. This promise was probably a political prerequisite of the intervention, and it is only after a month and more of bombing has failed to move the Serbs that political leaders are trying to crawl out from under it. We engaged ourselves, morally and politically, to provide the Kosovars with a technological fix, and if the fix didn't work, or didn't work quickly enough, we were ready (actually, as it turned out, not quite ready) to provide them with bread, blankets, and bandages. More than that, we said, we can't do. But there is something wrong here, for neither of these ways of helping is helpful enough. They don't meet the requirements of either politics or morality.

Maybe the bombing will eventually bring Milosevic down; maybe NATO will eventually decide to send in troops. But the initial form of the intervention raises a hard question. Are countries with armies whose soldiers cannot be put at risk morally or politically qualified to intervene? Even with a just cause and the best of intentions, how can we use military force in someone else's country unless we are prepared to deal with the unintended consequences of our actions? I suppose that had we been visibly ready in February or March to go into Kosovo on the ground, full-scale ethnic cleansing might have been forestalled. But that is too easy. Deterrence isn't effective unless the threat is plausible, and it's not clear at this moment that any of the Western democracies can pose a plausible threat.

We have armies that can't, or can't easily, be used. There are good democratic and even egalitarian reasons for this. Obviously,

U.S. national security is not at stake in Kosovo (nor is the security of any of the European nations, but I will focus now on the United States), and so it isn't possible to mobilize citizens to defend their homes and families. In other countries, in earlier times, wars in faraway places were fought by the lower orders or by mercenaries, people without political clout. But though the United States is still, even increasingly, an inegalitarian society, no soldier's mother or father is without political clout. This is an advance for Americans, since our political leaders cannot send soldiers into battle without convincing the country that the war is morally or politically necessary and that victory requires, and is worth, American lives. But there is an easier path for these same leaders. They can fight a war without using armies at all and so without convincing the country of the war's necessity. An easier path, which leads, however, to a moral anomaly: a new and dangerous inequality makes its appearance.

We are ready, apparently, to kill Serbian soldiers; we are ready to risk what is euphemistically called "collateral damage" to Serbian, and also to Kosovar, civilians. But we are not ready to send American soldiers into battle. Well, I have no love of battles, and I fully accept the obligation of democratically elected leaders to safeguard the lives of their own people, all of them. But this is not a possible moral position. *You can't kill unless you are prepared to die.* No doubt, that's a hard sentence — especially so because its two pronouns don't have the same reference (as they did when Albert Camus first made this argument, writing about assassination): the first "you" refers to the leaders of NATO, the second to the children of ordinary citizens. Still, these political leaders cannot launch a campaign aimed to kill Serbian soldiers, and sure to kill others too, unless they are prepared to risk the lives of their own soldiers. They can try, they ought to try, to reduce those risks as much as they can. But they cannot claim, we cannot accept, that those lives are expendable, and these not.

If the building is burning, and there are people inside, firefighters must risk their lives to get them out. That's what firefighters are for. But this isn't our building; those aren't our people. Why should we send in our firefighters? Americans can't be the world's firefighters.

This is a familiar argument, and not implausible, even though it often comes from people who don't seem to believe in putting out fires at all. I have heard it especially from people on the left (not only in America), and it is to them, especially, that I want to respond. Indeed, Milosevic should have been stopped years ago, when the first reports of ethnic cleansing came out of Bosnia. And he should have been stopped by the European powers. The Balkans is a European mess. Austro-Hungary carved out an empire there. Germany fought a war in Yugoslavia; Italians invaded Albania; the British armed Tito's partisans. There is a long history of military intervention and diplomatic intrigue. But today Europe as a military force exists only in alliance with the United States. That's not an eternal truth, and people who believe in international pluralism and a balance of power can hope for the emergence of an independent European Union with an army that it can put into action on its own. But it is true for now that no Kosovo intervention is possible without strong American involvement. If you want to stop Milosevic, you can argue about how to do it; there is no argument about who can do it.

That doesn't make us the world's firefighters. It was the Vietnamese who stopped Pol Pot in Cambodia, the Tanzanians who

KOSOVO

stopped Idi Amin in Uganda, the Indians who ended the killing
in East Pakistan, the Nigerians who went into Liberia. Some of
these were unilateral military acts, some (the Nigerian intervention, for example, and now the campaign in Kosovo) were authorized by regional alliances. Many people on the left yearn for a
world where the U.N., and only the U.N., would act in all such
cases. But given the oligarchic structure of the Security Council,
it's not possible to count on this kind of action: in most of the
cases on my list, U.N. intervention would have been vetoed by
one of the oligarchs. Nor am I convinced that the world would be
improved by having only one agent of international rescue. The
men and women in the burning building are probably better
served if they can appeal to more than a single set of firefighters.

But what is most important for the future of the left is that our
people, our activists and supporters around the world, see the
fires for what they are: deliberately set, the work of arsonists,
aimed to kill, terribly dangerous. Of course, every fire has a complicated social, political, and economic background. It would be
nice to understand it all. But once the burning begins something
less than full understanding is necessary: a will to put out the
fire — to find firefighters, close by if possible, and give them the
support they need. From a moral/political perspective, I don't
think it matters much if this particular fire isn't dangerous to me
and mine. I can't just sit and watch. Or rather, the price of sitting
and watching is a kind of moral corruption that leftists (and others too) must always resist.

THE *INTIFADA* AND THE GREEN LINE
(1988)

In Jerusalem in June a merchant on Ben Yehudah Street, in the western part of the city, complained to me about the collapse of tourism, the empty shops and hotels. She blamed the media for showing so many pictures of stone-throwing Palestinians and Israeli soldiers with clubs and tear gas. The pictures give a false impression: "Just look," she said, pointing to the street, "how peaceful it is." Indeed, Ben Yehudah Street was peaceful, lovely, noisy only with café conversations. The whole western part of the city was peaceful and lovely; the whole country, if one conceived the country in a certain way, was quiet. All the trouble was on the other side of the . . . what? The other side of the Green Line was suddenly the other side of the world. For years the government of Israel has claimed that the Green Line (Israel's border before the Six-Day War) did not exist. Erased from the map, it was also erased from the landscape, so that even adult Israelis, who had lived with the Line from 1948 until 1967, had difficulty visualizing exactly where it had been. But now the Palestinian *intifada* (uprising) has restored the Line, both on the ground and in the mind. The Line is what people are referring to when they say that the trouble is "on the other side."

The restoration of the Green Line is the major achievement of the *intifada*, and it is also the first condition of a settlement between Israel and the Palestinians. The Line today doesn't follow the old map; its exact location will one day have to be negotiated, and the negotiations, no doubt, will be difficult. But the *exact* location isn't terribly important. What is important is that the

Line is there and that it is known to be there. Its existential proof, so to speak, is the fact that Israelis travel "on the other side" armed, or with army protection, or at the invitation of the *intifada*. The Palestinians have demonstrated that they have a place of their own — which means that the occupation, however long it lasts, is only temporary. Yitzhak Shamir's government remains committed to a counterdemonstration; the harshness of the repression is designed to show that Israel is still in control of the occupied territories. So it is, mostly, but the control is now overtly and massively coercive, wholly different from the control the government exercises over the territory that is really its own, on "this side" of the Line. The difference between the homeland and the other land, whatever the ideologists of Greater Israel say, is plain to see. Though neither Palestinians nor Israelis are fully committed to it, partition has already begun.

Ever since the Begin government accelerated the pace of West Bank settlement, Israeli liberals and leftists have been haunted by the specter of communal war: Jews and Arabs, locked together geographically, economically, politically, not in trust but in suspicion and hate, endlessly terrorizing one another. The model was Northern Ireland or Lebanon, and one could already see the Lebanization of Israel in those awful funerals where one speaker after another called for revenge (Hebrew and Arabic sound very much alike on such occasions) tenfold, a hundredfold. Every death was a new provocation. But the *intifada*, though there have been funerals enough, is not communal war — at least, it is nothing at all like Ireland or Lebanon. For in those countries the "warriors" are individuals or gangs whose "warfare" consists of assassination, murder, kidnapping, hijacking, car bombing, and so on; the warring communities are themselves passive, disorganized, victimized. By contrast, the *intifada* is sustained by a genuinely *national* mobilization, and so it holds forth the promise (at last) of a new nation. What PLO terrorists failed to achieve over 20 years, teenagers with slingshots have achieved in eight months. They have put Palestine on the moral map, alongside Israel.

I don't mean to romanticize the *intifada*. Like all political violence, it is marked by its own coerciveness, its own brutality and fanaticism. But, as even Yitzhak Rabin has recognized, it is not terrorist in character. The youngsters who do the everyday work of the uprising are not a specially trained cadre of killers. They are everyone's children, and they are supported by a full-scale popular movement and by an extraordinary network of local committees. The problem with the movement and its network is that they have not yet produced an external politics. They speak to Israel only with stones, not with words, not with arguments, proposals, visions of the future. That's why the restoration of the Green Line isn't yet a settlement; it needs to be confirmed in negotiation — and the confirmation is resisted on both sides of the Line.

So the second condition of a peace settlement is mutual recognition, the acknowledgment by each side of the moral legitimacy, which is to say, the *nationhood*, of the other. The two recognitions must be symmetrical, certainly, but at the same time they serve different purposes; they have different meanings and practical entailments for Israeli Jews and Palestinian Arabs. To put it simply, and no doubt crudely, the Jews need recognition because of their vulnerability, the Palestinians because of their humiliation. I learned long ago to be skeptical about national psychologies and collective psychoanalysis, and so I hasten to add that these are by no means the needs of every Jew or of every Palestinian. They are nonetheless morally obvious and politically unavoidable.

For the Palestinians, the years of occupation have been years of disgrace — all the more so since the occupation, until last December, was so easy for Israel. Most of the Palestinians in the territories were passive, seemingly incapable of self-help, effectively collaborating in their own subjection. The mobilization that began in December has made them proud, as any number of terrorist "victories" could not do. Indeed, the *intifada* is for the Palestinians what the crossing of the Suez Canal was in 1973 for the Egyptians, and its psychological effects could well survive, in the first case as in the second, a military defeat or repression. Here is a possible foundation for political compromise. But the compromise will have to incorporate and institutionalize the new Palestinian pride. That is what underlies the demand for self-determination and gives it meaning. Terrorists cannot claim a right to self-determination; a popular movement can, and the Palestinians have finally produced a popular movement.

How self-determination might work, what its outcome might be — these things are as uncertain as ever. The *intifada* settles nothing; it is still possible to imagine a range of negotiating strategies, a variety of representatives, a number of alternative "arrangements" at the end. But there can't be a settlement, now, that isn't acceptable to the Palestinians of the West Bank and Gaza. That probably rules out an Israeli deal with King Hussein, as the king himself seems to have recognized — though he may yet return as a partner of the Palestinians or as a guarantor of the eventual settlement. It probably requires a deal with the PLO, though the PLO might well act through representatives from the West Bank and Gaza, who have been licensed, so to speak, by the local committees.

Israelis talk about Palestinian pride with a mixture of anxiety and admiration. The response of the government, however, has been less equivocal: it has aimed not only to defeat the uprising but to force the Palestinians to acknowledge defeat — "to wipe the smile off the Palestinian face," as one official is reported to have said. Anxiety and admiration are much healthier responses: anxiety because pride can feed an extremist politics as easily as it can ground a moderate politics; admiration because Israeli history too, as it is commonly told, is a tale of triumph over humiliation — the defenseless ghetto Jew transformed into the self-confident *sabra*. Israelis of roughly my age remember throwing stones at British soldiers. It is a useful, if also a disturbing, memory.

Because of memories like this, the recognition that Israel requires doesn't have much to do with honor. Israelis have already experienced the exhilarations of communal discipline and self-help. But Israel's Jewish citizens have other memories, haunting memories of persecution, exile, war, and death. When Prime Minister Shamir says of the *intifada* that it is a new form of warfare against the State of Israel, as if children with slingshots pose a threat to the very existence of the state, he is saying something absurd. But the absurdity is widely accepted — for haven't the Arabs been at war with Israel for 40 years now, always refusing (Egypt the only exception) to accept Israeli statehood? Similarly, the reiterated refrain of right-wing political rhetoric, "everyone is against us," is quite simply untrue. But it too is widely accepted, for it resonates with the historical experience of the Jewish people. The Zionist achievement — statehood, material power, political alliances, and standing in the world — can't yet be fully appreciated by its own protagonists and beneficiaries, though it is certainly appreciated by the Palestinians, who want desperately to imitate it. For all their military strength, Israelis feel terribly vulnerable. What they want from recognition is security.

In material terms, security means defensible borders, demilitarization, electronic warning stations, and so on. The arrangements in the Sinai provide useful precedents. But Israel requires something more, as Sadat understood very clearly (and as Arafat seems incapable of understanding): it requires public recognition by the Arabs of its need for security and of its right to defend its sovereignty. Western diplomats call upon the PLO to recognize the existence of Israel. But that is too easy — plague and war also "exist," and we recognize their existence precisely in order to get rid of them if we possibly can. The PLO must find some way of saying that it has finally and forever given up its hope of getting rid of Israel. That is the necessary moral background to this or that set of security arrangements. Without that, the arrangements won't be believable to most Israeli Jews.

It appears today that there are factions in the PLO that are prepared to make the necessary public statements; there are also factions committed to eternal war. The PLO is not a coherent political organization. Perhaps it can only become a coherent organization in the course of a negotiating process, when it is forced to make practical decisions. Perhaps the very decision to join a negotiating process would force upon Arafat his own version of an "Altalena affair" (in which David Ben-Gurion, in 1948, forcibly suppressed the right-wing Irgun, led by Menachem Begin). In any case, right now there is no Palestinian leadership capable of doing what Sadat did in 1977. At that time, the ceremonies of recognition — the visit to Jerusalem, the Knesset speech — preceded the formal negotiations; now they will almost certainly come, if they come at all, afterward.

How, then, might the negotiations get started? I am inclined to think that they won't get started without a great power agreement. Russia and the United States can provide a substitute of sorts (though only a temporary one) for the mutual recognition of Israelis and Palestinians — Russian recognition giving the Israelis a sense that their sovereignty is now beyond challenge; American recognition giving the Palestinians a sense that they are on their way to a sovereignty of their own. This is the third condition of a settlement, and it requires a great deal more diplomatic cooperation between the great powers — and skill and verve on both sides — than either has yet shown itself ready for.

The ineffectiveness of American diplomacy is revealed in two recent incidents. First, Shamir's visit to Washington in March (already the fourth month of the *intifada*), where he smiled and smiled, rejected every American proposal, escaped unscathed — and reaped substantial political benefits from the escape. Second, the arrival in Washington in June (the seventh month) of the Abu Sharif "document," which seemed to acknowledge Israel's legitimacy and even, maybe, its security needs, but which was never itself acknowledged by Arafat and was soon denounced by his second-in-command. These were, on both sides, the games of the irreconcilables. It is a sign of Washington's potential power that the games focus on Washington; that the games go on at all is a sign of its inability to use that power effectively. I suspect that American power can't be used effectively unless it is shared to some degree with the Russians. For the United States will not be able to (and in any case should not) bring pressure to bear on Israel or begin its own discussions with the PLO until the Russians have demonstrated their readiness to disown those forces in the Arab world committed to Israel's destruction.

Then the serious negotiations might begin. And the fourth and final condition of a settlement is a *long* negotiating process. We should expect a long process simply because of the high stakes and the complexity of the issues. There were, remember, two years of on and off negotiations between Sadat's visit to Jerusalem and the actual signing of an Egyptian-Israeli peace treaty—and that agreement was easy compared with what remains to be done. But even if some understanding of the necessary final arrangements came quickly into view, it would be useful to drag out the talks. For both sides need time to accustom themselves to the idea of peace and to the compromises, and therefore the ideological losses, that it involves.

For the Jews, peace means the end of Greater Israel and of the messianic hopes that a small but fervent faction of religious and nationalist zealots associates with territorial "greatness." It means adjusting to the physical as well as the mental constraints of a very little country. With the re-establishment of the Green Line, this adjustment has already begun, though no Israeli leader has yet emerged who can cast it in a positive light. No doubt peace with the Palestinians would be a great Zionist victory, for it would represent the definitive establishment of the Jewish state. The question is whether it would feel that way, and this question can only be answered over a period of time during which ordinary Israelis can test the Palestinian commitment to a genuine settlement.

For the Palestinians, peace means the acceptance of a "Palestine" that is even littler (unless it is associated in some way with Jordan) than little Israel. That will be especially difficult for the Palestinian diaspora, which remains dominant, despite the *intifada*, within the PLO. It is still not clear that the leadership of the PLO really wants a West Bank and Gazan ministate: they have missed so many opportunities to move toward that goal that one cannot help wondering whether they don't still have other goals in mind. The effective surrender of these other goals won't take place at a single moment in time, though Hussein's divorce decree brings the time much nearer when the Palestinians must say exactly what it is they hope to win. This will probably require bloody fights as well as arguments within the PLO, and it will be best if the fights take place before rather than after the final settlement — for the sake of that finality. At some point the surrender of the maximalists will have to find public expression, and some Palestinian leader will have to explain to his people why it is really a victory. Perhaps the only person who can do that will be someone who already has a stake in the success of the negotiating process.

This is what politics is often like: it is a muddle for a long time, and the necessary clarity is finally achieved only because of the muddle. But do the conditions exist, in fact, for this sort of muddling through? I can't say that they do; the safest prediction about the future is a grim one: stalemate rather than settlement, the *intifada* matched but not beaten by the repression. Mutual recognition and coexistence are explicitly defended only by a minority of Israeli Jews and by a much smaller (and less well organized) minority of Palestinian Arabs. And the power of the great powers isn't at this moment intelligently or cooperatively deployed. Only the Green Line is there again, awaiting formal confirmation. But we can now see what the conditions of a settlement are. It is important to keep them steadily in view.

The great simplifiers are hard at work, but Israel/Palestine has
never been a friendly environment for them, and it is especially
unfriendly today. They are bound to get it wrong, morally and
politically, and that is a very bad thing to do, for the stakes are
high. There isn't one war going on in the Middle East, and there
isn't a single opposition of right and wrong, just and unjust. Four
Israeli-Palestinian wars are now in progress.

- The first is a Palestinian war to destroy the state of Israel.
- The second is a Palestinian war to create an independent
  state alongside Israel, ending the occupation of the West
  Bank and Gaza.
- The third is an Israeli war for the security of Israel within
  the 1967 borders.
- The fourth is an Israeli war for Greater Israel, for the settle-
  ments and the occupied territories.

It isn't easy to say which war is being fought at any given
moment; in a sense, the four are simultaneous. They are also
continuous; the wars go on even when the fighting stops, as if in
confirmation of Thomas Hobbes's definition: "For war consist-
eth not in battle only, or the act of fighting, but in a tract of time
wherein the will to contend by battle is sufficiently known. . . . "
Throughout the course of the Oslo peace process, some Palestinians and some Israelis were fighting the first and fourth of these
wars — or, at least, were committed to fighting them (and their
will to contend was sufficiently known so that it could have been

dealt with). The actual decision to restart the battles was taken by the Palestinians in September 2000; since then, all four wars have been actively in progress.

Different people are fighting each of the four wars at the same time, side by side, though the overall emphasis falls differently at different times. Our moral and political judgments have to reflect this complexity. Taken separately, two of the wars are just and two are unjust. But they don't appear separately in the "real world." For analytic purposes, we can begin by looking at them one by one, but we won't be able to stop there.

1. *The war against Israel:* this is the war that is "declared" every time a terrorist attacks Israeli civilians. I believe that terrorism always announces a radical devaluation of the people who are targeted for random murder: Irish Protestants in the heyday of the IRA, Europeans in Algeria during the National Liberation Front's (FLN) campaign for independence, Americans on September 11. Whatever individual terrorists say about their activities, the intention that they signal to the world, and above all to their victims, is radical and frightening: a politics of massacre or removal or of overthrow and subjugation. Terrorism isn't best understood as a negotiating strategy; it aims instead at total victory, unconditional surrender. The flight of a million and a half Europeans from Algeria was exactly the sort of victory that terrorists seek (the FLN was helped in its project, it should be remembered, by terrorists on the European side).

Israel's Jewish citizens have to assume that something similar is what Palestinian terrorists are seeking today: the end of the Jewish state, the removal of the Jews. The language of incitement — the sermons in Palestinian mosques, the funerals where the "martyrdom" of suicide bombers is commemorated, the slogans shouted at political demonstrations, the celebration of terrorists as heroes in schools run by the Palestine Authority (PA) — makes this intention clear, and it is the explicit goal of the leading terrorist organizations, Hamas and Islamic Jihad. But can it be called the goal of the Palestinian liberation movement taken as a whole? Is this what Yasir Arafat is really after? It isn't easy to read him; he may think that he is using the terrorists; he may even hope one day to kill or exile them as the Algerian government did to its terrorists in the aftermath of independence. But clearly, whatever his ultimate intentions, he is right now a supporter or at least an accomplice of terrorism. His distancing gestures, the occasional arrests, and the perfunctory condemnations after each attack long ago ceased to be convincing; he cannot be surprised if ordinary Israelis feel radically threatened. This first war is a real war, even if it looks right now like a losing war with terrible consequences for the Palestinian people and even if some (or many) Palestinians believe themselves to be fighting a different war.

2. *The war for an independent state:* this is the war that leftist sympathizers in Europe and America commonly claim that the Palestinians are fighting, because they think that this is the war the Palestinians should be fighting. And some (or many) of them are. The Palestinians need a state. Before 1967, they needed a state to protect them against Egypt (in Gaza) and Jordan (on the West Bank); since 1967, they need a state to protect them against Israel. I have no doubt about this, nor about the Palestinian right to the state they need, even though I believe that the original seizure of the West Bank and Gaza was justified. In 1967, the Arabs were fighting a war of the first kind on my list, against the very existence of Israel. There was no occupation in those days; Egyptian publicists talked openly of driving the Jews "into the

sea." But the territories that Israel controlled at the end of its victorious defense were supposed to be used (this is what its leaders said at the time) as bargaining chips toward a future peace. When, instead, the government sponsored and supported settlements beyond the old border (the Green Line), it conferred legitimacy on a resistance movement aimed at liberation. And the longer the occupation went on, the more settlements proliferated and expanded, the more land was expropriated and water rights seized, the stronger that movement grew. It is worth recalling how peaceful the occupation was in its early days, how few soldiers it required when it was believed, on both sides, to be temporary (and when war number one had been decisively defeated). A decade later, Prime Minister Menachem Begin denied that there was any such thing as "occupied territory"; the whole land was the Land of Israel; the government adopted the ideology of conquest and settlement. And the occupation was far more onerous, far more oppressive when its reality was denied than when it was called by its true name.

So it is certainly a legitimate goal of Palestinian militants to establish a state of their own, free of Israel — and of Egypt and Jordan too. The first *intifada* (1987), with its stone-throwing children, looked like a struggle for a state of this kind, limited to the West Bank and Gaza, where the children lived. It was not exactly a nonviolent struggle (though it was sometimes described that way by people who weren't watching), but it did show discipline and high morale, and its protagonists seemed to acknowledge limits to their struggle: it wasn't intended to threaten Israelis on their side of the Green Line, where most Israelis lived [see the previous chapter (8)]. And that is why it was successful in advancing the peace process — though Palestinian leaders subsequently declined, so it seems to me, to gather the fruits of their success.

The renewed *intifada* that began in the fall of 2000 is a violent struggle, and it is not confined to the Occupied Territories. Still, the interviews that journalists have conducted with many of the fighters suggest that they (or some of them) consider themselves to be fighting to end the occupation and force the settlers to leave; their aim is an independent state alongside Israel. So this second war is a real war too, though again it isn't clear that Arafat is committed to it. Does he want what some, at least, of his people certainly want: a small state alongside a small (but not as small) Israeli state? Does he want to trade in the aura of heroic struggle for the routine drudgery of state-building? Does he want to worry about the water supply in Jericho and the development of an industrial zone in Nablus? If the answer to these questions is yes, then we should all hope that Arafat gets what he wants. The problem is that many Israelis, who would share this hope if they were hopeful about anything, don't believe, and don't have much reason to believe, that the answer is yes.

3. *The war for Israeli security:* it is unclear how many Israeli soldiers think that this is the war they are fighting, but the number is certainly high. The reserve call-up that preceded the March-April 2002 Israeli "incursions" into West Bank cities and towns produced a startling result. Usually the army calls up about twice the number of soldiers that it needs; the routine pressures of civilian life — sick children, infirm parents, school exams, trouble at the office — are accepted as excuses; lots of reservists don't show up. In March 2002, more than 95 percent of them did show up. These people did not believe that they were fighting for the occupied territories and the settlements; all the opinion polls

show a massive unwillingness to do that. They believed that they were fighting for their country or, perhaps better, for their safety and survival in their country. The 95 percent response was the direct product of the terrorist attacks. It is possible, of course, that Sharon exploited the fear of terrorism in order to fight a different war than the one his soldiers thought they were fighting. Still, whatever the war in Sharon's mind, a substantial part of the Israeli army was defending the country against the terrorist threat. The third war is a real war and, morally, a very important war: a defense of home and family in the most immediate sense. But some Israeli homes and families are located on the wrong side of the Green Line, where their defense is morally problematic.

4. *The war for the Occupied Territories:* the Israeli right is definitely committed to this war, but the support they have in the country is (again) uncertain. Prime Minister Ehud Barak at Camp David in 2000 believed that he would win a referendum for an almost total withdrawal, if this were part of a negotiated settlement of the conflict as a whole. Withdrawal under pressure of terrorist attacks probably does not have similar support, but that tells us nothing about the extent of support for the occupation and the settlements; it tells us only that Palestinian terrorism is a political disaster for the Israeli left. In the face of terror, the left cannot mobilize opposition to the settlements; it finds itself marginalized; its potential supporters are more and more skeptical about its central claim: that withdrawal from the territories would bring a real peace. And that skepticism opens the way for right-wing politicians to defend the settlements — which are no different, they argue, from cities and towns on the Israeli side of the Green Line: if we don't fight for Ariel and Kiryat Arbah (Jewish towns on the West Bank), we will have to fight for Tel Aviv and Haifa.

But the fight for Ariel and Kiryat Arbah guarantees that there won't be a real peace. For the settler movement is the functional equivalent of the terrorist organizations. I hasten to add that it is *not the moral equivalent.* The settlers are not murderers, even if there are a small number of terrorists among them. But the message of settler activity to the Palestinians is very much like the message of terrorism to the Israelis: we want you to leave (some groups on the Israeli right, including groups represented in Sharon's government, openly support a policy of "transfer"), or we want you to accept a radically subordinate position in your own country. The settlers' aim is Greater Israel, and the achievement of that aim would mean that there could not be a Palestinian state. It is in this sense only that they are like the terrorists: they want the whole thing. They are prepared to fight for the whole thing, and some Israelis presumably believe that that is what they are doing right now. The fourth war is a real war. The vote of the Likud in May 2002 to bar any future Israeli government from accepting a Palestinian state suggests a strong commitment to continue the occupation and enlarge the settlements. Still, I suspect that most of the reservists called up in March, or those who are now (August) patrolling Palestinian cities, would not be prepared to fight for those goals if they thought that this was the only war in which they were engaged.

It was the great mistake of the two center-left prime ministers, Yitzhak Rabin and Barak, not to set themselves against the settler movement from the beginning. They thought that they would most easily defeat the right-wing supporters of Greater Israel if they waited until the very end of the peace process. Meanwhile they compromised with the right and allowed a steady growth in the number of settlers. If, instead, they had frozen settlement activity and chosen a few isolated settlements to dismantle, they would have provoked a political battle that I am sure they would have won; and that victory would have been definitive; a gradual out-migration of settler families from the territories would have begun. Failing that, Palestinian radicals were able to convince many of their people that compromise was impossible; the conflict could have only one ending: either the Palestinians or the Israelis would have to go.

The right responds by claiming that this was always the view of Palestinian radicals, even before there were any settlements beyond the old border. And that is certainly true: the radicals object to Jewish sovereignty on any part of "Arab" territory; they have no interest in the Green Line. But the supporters of the settlers, especially the religious supporters, are radical in exactly the same way. They also have no interest in the Green Line; they oppose Arab sovereignty on any part of the land that historically or by divine gift "belongs" to the Jewish people. The aim of the fourth war is to enforce this conception of belonging.

I need to say something about the "right of return," even though the refugees who claim this right, since they mostly live beyond the borders of old Palestine, are not directly involved in any of the four wars. Still, they may well be the crucial constituency for war number one. Arafat's insistence that return is a make-or-break issue must be directed in part at them; he has always drawn support from the Palestinian diaspora. "Return" was probably a crucial factor in the failure of the Camp David negotiations in the late summer of 2000. Here, however, there is disagreement among the participants: was Arafat insisting on a symbolic acceptance of the right or on an actual return? Most Israelis choose to be literal-minded about this, arguing that acceptance of the right would open the way to the return of hundreds of thousands of Palestinians, overwhelming the current Jewish majority. Return, they claim, means two Palestinian states. Most Palestinians argue for the importance of the symbolism and seem eager to postpone any discussion of numbers. At Taba in January 2001 both sides did talk about numbers and, apparently, the figures suggested by the two were very far apart.

Among Palestinians, only Sari Nuseibeh, the PA's representative in Jerusalem, has been ready to argue that giving up the right of return is the necessary price of statehood. That seems to me the right position, since the claim to return effectively reopens the 1947–1948 conflict, which is not a helpful thing to do more than half a century later. All the other refugees from the years immediately after World War Two, from Central Europe to Southeast Asia, have been successfully resettled. Palestinians are still in camps because a decision was made, by their own leaders and by the adjacent Arab states, to keep them there: this was a way of insisting that Israel's independence war was not yet over. Today, however, if the Palestinians are to win their own independence war, they must acknowledge that Israel's is already won. Perhaps some number of refugees will return to Israel, some greater number to Palestine (how many will depend on the pace of investment and economic development). The rest must finally be resettled. It is time to address their actual misery rather than their symbolic claims. There will continue to be a Palestinian diaspora, just as there continues to be a Jewish diaspora. A clear statement by Arafat acknowledging this simple truth would represent a big step toward undeclaring the first war.

How can we adjudicate among the four wars? What kind of judgments can we make about whom to support or oppose, and when? A lot depends on the questions I have not answered: how many Israelis, how many Palestinians, endorse each of the wars? Or, perhaps better, we might ask: what would happen if each side won its own just war? If the Palestinians were able to create a state on their side of the Green Line, would they (or a sufficient majority of them) regard that as the fulfillment of their national aspirations? Would they accept that kind of statehood as the end of the conflict, or would the new state sponsor an irredentist politics and secretly collude in an ongoing terrorist war? Arafat's behavior at Camp David and after doesn't suggest a hopeful answer to these questions. Similarly, does the Israeli defense of statehood stop at the Green Line, or does the current government's conception of state security (or historical destiny) require territories beyond that, even far beyond that? Sharon's behavior since coming to power doesn't suggest a hopeful answer to this question.

What happened at Camp David is obviously important in shaping our moral judgments of the two sides and the four wars, for it was Barak's inability to conclude an agreement there that sealed his fate and brought Sharon to power. Arafat refused to make peace and survived; Barak failed to make peace and was defeated (we can learn something about the constituencies of the two men from this contrast). It is true that the state of the negotiations and the proposals on the table at Camp David and Taba are still in dispute. The people who were at the table disagree among themselves; I have no private information to bring to this argument. But it seems reasonably clear that each successive move in the negotiating process brought the Palestinians nearer to statehood and sovereign control over something close to (and with each move closer to) the whole of the territories. The claim that the Palestinians were offered nothing more than a disconnected set of "Bantustans" seems to be false; an almost fully connected Palestine (the West Bank and Gaza would still have been separate territories) was at least a possible and even a likely outcome of the ongoing negotiations, whatever was actually offered at this or that moment. So the decision to walk away from the process and to begin, and then to militarize, the second intifada is very hard to understand — especially hard because we have to assume that Arafat knew that Palestinian violence guaranteed the defeat of Barak's center-left government. It isn't a crazy conclusion that he simply wasn't interested in or, when the critical moment came, wasn't prepared for a historic compromise and an end to the conflict — even if the compromise brought with it a sovereign state on the West Bank and Gaza.

Hence the order of the four wars in my presentation. I put war number one, for the destruction of the state of Israel, ahead of war number two, for statehood in the territories, because it appears that statehood could have been achieved without any war at all. And I put the war for Greater Israel after the defensive war for Israeli security because the previous Israeli government was prepared to renounce territorial "greatness" entirely. But if the Palestinians make a serious effort to repress the terrorist organizations, and if that effort does not move the Sharon government to rethink its position on the territories, then these orderings would have to be revised. In any case, all four wars are now in progress: what can we say about them?

The first war has to be defeated or definitively renounced. Critics of Israel in Europe and at the United Nations have made a terrible mistake, a moral as well as a political mistake, in failing to acknowledge the necessity of this defeat. They have condemned each successive terrorist attack on Israeli civilians, often in stronger language than Arafat has used, but they have not recognized, let alone condemned, the succession itself, the attacks taken together, as an unjust war against the very existence of Israel. There have been too many excuses for terrorism, too many efforts to "understand" terror as a response (terrible, of course) to the oppressiveness of the occupation. It is likely, indeed, that some terrorists are motivated by personal encounters with the occupying forces or by a more general sense of the humiliation of being occupied. But many other people have responded differently to the same experience: there is an ongoing argument among Palestinians (as there was in the IRA and the Algerian FLN) about the usefulness and moral legitimacy of terror. Palestinian sympathizers on the European left and elsewhere should be very careful not to join this argument on the side of the terrorists.

Winning the second war, for the establishment of a Palestinian state, depends on losing or renouncing the first. That dependence, it seems to me, is morally clear; it hasn't always been politically clear. If there ever is a foreign intervention in the Israeli/Palestinian conflict, one of its goals should be to clarify the relationship of the first and second wars (and also of the third and fourth). The Palestinians can have a state only when they make it clear to the Israelis that the state they want is one that stands alongside Israel. At some point, a Palestinian leader (it is unlikely to be Arafat) will have to do what Anwar Sadat did in 1977: welcome Israel as a Middle Eastern neighbor. Since Israel already exists, and Palestine doesn't, one might expect the welcome to come from the other direction. Perhaps it should; at some point, certainly, the welcome must be mutual. But the extent of the terror attacks now requires the Palestinians to find some convincing way to repudiate the slogan that still echoes at their demonstrations: "Kill the Jews!"

The relation of the third and fourth wars is symmetrical to that of the first and second: war number four, for Greater Israel, must be lost or definitively renounced if war number three, for Israel itself, is to be won. The March–April 2002 attacks on West Bank cities, and the return of Israeli soldiers to those same cities in June–July, would be much easier to defend if it was clear that the aim was not to maintain the occupation but only to end or reduce the terrorist threat. In the absence of a Palestinian war on terror, an Israeli war is certainly justifiable. No state can fail to defend the lives of its citizens (that's what states are for). But it was a morally necessary prelude to that war that the Sharon government declare its political commitment to end the occupation and bring the settlers home (many of them, at least: the actual number will depend on a negotiated agreement on final borders for the two states). Perhaps U.N. officials would have condemned the Israeli war anyway, whatever the government's declared commitments, but the condemnations could then have been seen as acts of hostility — not to be confused with serious moral judgments. As it was, the fierce argument about the massacre-that-never-happened in Jenin obscured the real moral issue, which was not the conduct of the battles but the political vision of the government that ordered them. The conduct of the battles seems to have conformed to the standards of just war theory, though the use of air power (for example, against the Gaza apartment house in July) has not always done so. The current occupation of Palestinian cities and the practice of collective punishment impose unjustifiable hardships on the civilian population. In battle, however, the Israeli army regularly accepted risks to its own men in order to reduce the risks that it imposed on the civilian population. The contrast with the way the Russians fought in Grozny, to take the most recent example of large-scale urban warfare, is striking, and the crucial mark of that contrast is the very small number of civilian casualties in the Palestinian cities despite the fierceness of the fighting. But the legitimacy of Israeli self-defense will finally be determined by the size of the "self" — the extent of the territory — that is being defended.

Almost everybody has a peace plan: one peace for the four wars. And everybody's plan (leaving aside those Palestinians and Israelis who are fighting for the whole thing) is more or less the same. There have to be two states, divided by a border close to the Green Line, with changes mutually agreed upon. How to get there, and how to make sure that both sides stay there once they get there — on these questions the disagreements are profound, between Palestinians and Israelis and also within both groups. Except in the most general terms, I cannot address these questions. The general terms are clear enough: Palestinians must renounce terrorism; Israelis must renounce occupation. In fact, neither renunciation seems likely given the existing leadership of the two sides. But there is a significant peace movement in Israel, and several political parties committed to renunciation, and among the Palestinians, though no comparable movement exists, there are at least small signs of opposition to the terror attacks. Perhaps whatever forward movement is possible must come independently from the two sides and, first of all, from outside what we used to call the "ruling circles."

What follows is a hard argument, and I don't make it with any confidence. I shall simply repeat what some of my friends in the

Israeli peace movement are now saying (I can't speak for Palestinian oppositionists). They argue that there is a way to defend Israeli citizens and to signal, at the same time, a readiness to return to some modified version of the 1967 border. A unilateral withdrawal from isolated settlements in Gaza and the West Bank would instantly improve Israel's defensive position, shortening the lines that the army has to patrol, and it would provoke the political battle with the settlers that (as I have already argued) should have been fought years ago. In the near future, this withdrawal is more likely to take shape as a leftist program than as a government policy, but it would still begin the necessary battle inside Israel, and it might encourage Palestinian oppositionists to begin a battle of their own: a serious effort to rein in the terrorist organizations so that the Israeli withdrawal, when it finally comes, does not generate a wave of enthusiasm among the militants and then a series of new attacks. That prospect is the obvious danger of any unilateralism, and it is a real danger, as the withdrawal from Lebanon demonstrates. But the risk might still be worth taking.

Ultimately, the partisans of wars two and three must defeat the partisans of wars one and four. The way to peace begins with these two internal (but not necessarily uncoordinated) battles. An American or American/European-sponsored truce would help the moderates on both sides, but, at the same time, the success of the truce depends on the strength of the moderates. Right now, it is hard to judge whether the "reform" of the Palestinian Authority would increase that strength. All good things don't come together in political life: some of the most moderate Palestinians are among the most corrupt, while the suicide bombers are no doubt idealists. Democratic elections in Palestine may well play into the hands of nationalist and religious demagogues; this is a real possibility in Israel too. Still, a more open politics among the Palestinians would allow public expressions of support for a compromise peace, and that would be a major advance.

Would it help to bring in an international force, under U.N. auspices, to police the (temporary or permanent) lines between Israel and Palestine? This is an increasingly popular idea, but it raises difficult questions about reciprocity. The Israeli settlers would have to be defeated before any such force came in, because the border along which it was deployed would certainly exclude many of the existing settlements. But the Palestinian terrorists would not have to be defeated, because they sit comfortably on one side of the line. It is easy to predict what would happen next: terrorists will slip through the U.N.'s multinational patrols and kill Israeli civilians. Then Israel will demand that U.N. soldiers go after the terrorist organizations, which, since that would involve a major military campaign, they would refuse to do. And what then? An international force prepared to use force (and accept casualties) might well bring peace to the Middle East, but I cannot think of any country that is seriously prepared to commit its soldiers to actual battles. The U.N.'s record in Bosnia, Rwanda, and East Timor is appalling. So, the only force likely to be deployed is one organized for peacekeeping, not peacemaking, and then its effectiveness will depend on the previous victory of Israeli and Palestinian moderates. Internationalization is no substitute for that victory, and it is certainly doomed to failure if it follows upon the victory of Israeli moderates only.

There is a form of international engagement, more ideological and political than military, that could be genuinely helpful. It is critically important to delegitimize the terrorists and the settlers.

But this has to be done simultaneously and with some modicum of moral intelligence. The current boycott campaign against Israel, modeled on the 1980s campaign against South Africa, aims at a very one-sided delegitimation. And because the other side isn't led by an organization remotely like the African National Congress, or by a man remotely like Nelson Mandela, the success of this campaign would be disastrous. It would strengthen the forces fighting the first war. Only when European critics of Israel are prepared to tell the Palestinians that there will be no help for a PA complicit in terrorism, can they ask American critics of the Palestinians to deliver a parallel message to the Israeli government. Intellectuals committed to internationalism can best serve their cause by explaining and defending the two messages together.

I have tried to reflect the complexity of the Israeli/Palestinian conflict. I cannot pretend to perfect objectivity. The Israeli nationalist right, even the religious right, is a familiar enemy for me, whereas the ideology of death and martyrdom endorsed by so many Palestinians today is alien; I don't understand it. So perhaps someone else could provide a more adequate account of the four wars. What is crucial is to acknowledge the four. Most commentators, especially on the European left, but also on the Jewish and Christian right here in the United States, have failed to do that, producing instead ideological caricatures of the conflict. The caricatures would be easy to ridicule, if they did not have such deadly effects. For they encourage Palestinians and Israelis to fight the first and fourth wars. Those of us who watch and worry about the Middle East have at least an obligation not to do that.

AFTER 9/11: FIVE QUESTIONS ABOUT TERRORISM

(2002)

This is not going to be a straightforward and entirely coherent argument. I am still reeling from the attacks of September 11, and I don't have all my responses in order. I will try to answer five questions about terrorism. Whether the answers add up to a "position" — theoretical or practical — I will leave to the reader.

1. What is terrorism?
2. How should we go about explaining it?
3. How is it defended or excused?
4. How should we respond?
5. What will be the signs of a successful response?

1. *What is it?* It's not hard to recognize; we can safely avoid postmodernist arguments about knowledge and truth. Terrorism is the deliberate killing of innocent people, at random, in order to spread fear through a whole population and force the hand of its political leaders. But this is a definition that best fits the terrorism of a national liberation or revolutionary movement (the Irish Republican Army, the Algerian National Liberation Front [FLN], the Palestine Liberation Organization, the Basque Separatist Movement, and so on). There is also state terrorism, commonly used by authoritarian and totalitarian governments against their own people, to spread fear and make political opposition impossible: the Argentine "disappearances" are a useful example. And, finally, there is war terrorism: the effort to kill civilians in such large numbers that their government is forced to surrender. Hiroshima seems to me the classic case. The common element is the targeting of people who are, in both the military and political

senses, noncombatants: not soldiers, not public officials, just ordinary people. And they aren't killed incidentally in the course of
actions aimed elsewhere; they are killed intentionally.

I don't accept the notion that "one man's terrorist is another
man's freedom fighter." Of course, the use of the term is contested; that's true of many political terms. The use of "democracy" is contested, but we still have, I think, a pretty good idea of
what democracy is (and isn't). When communist Bulgaria called
itself a "people's democracy," only fools were fooled. The case is
the same with terrorism. In the 1960s, when someone from the
FLN put a bomb in a café where French teenagers gathered to
flirt and dance and called himself a freedom fighter, only fools
were fooled. There were a lot of fools back then, and back then —
in the sixties and seventies — was when the culture of excuse and
apology was born (but I want to deal with that later).

2. *How should we go about explaining terrorism — and particularly
the form of terrorism that we face today?* The first thing to understand is that terrorism is a choice; it is a political strategy selected
from among a range of options. You have to imagine [see Chapter 4] a group of people sitting around a table and arguing about
what to do; the moment is hard to reconstruct, but I am sure that
it is an actual moment, even if, once the choice is made, the
people who opposed terror are commonly killed, and so we never
hear their version of how the argument went. Why do the terrorists so often win the argument? What are the political roots of
terror?

I don't think that a simple materialist explanation works,
though there has been a lot of talk in the last couple of months
about the human misery, the terrible poverty, the vast global
inequalities in which terrorism is "ultimately rooted." Also about

the terrible suffering, as someone wrote in one of our weeklies, endured by "people all over the world who have been the victims of American military action — in Vietnam, in Latin America, in Iraq . . ." The author of those words doesn't seem to have noticed that there are no terrorists coming from Vietnam and Latin America. Misery and inequality just don't work as explanations for any of the nationalist terrorist movements and certainly not for Islamic terror. A simple thought experiment in comparative politics helps explain why they don't work. Surely it is Africa that reveals the worst consequences of global inequality, and the involvement of the West in the production and reproduction of inequality is nowhere more evident. There is a lot of local involvement too; many African governments are complicitous or directly responsible for the misery of their own people. Still, the role of the West is fairly large. And yet the African diaspora is not a friendly sea in which terrorists swim. And the same thing can be said for Latin America, especially Central America, where U.S. companies have played a significant part in exploiting and sustaining poverty: and yet the Latin diaspora is not a friendly sea. We need another explanation.

We need a combined cultural-religious-political explanation that has to focus, I think, on the creation of an Enemy, a whole people who are ideologically or theologically degraded so that they are available for murder: that's what the IRA did to Irish Protestants, the FLN to French Algerians, the PLO to Israeli Jews. This kind of Enemy is the special creation of nationalist and religious movements, which often aim not only at the defeat but at the removal or elimination of the "others." Wartime propaganda commonly has the same effect, demonizing the other side, even when both sides expect the war to end with a negotiated peace. Once the Enemy has been created, any of "them" can be killed, men, women, or children, combatants and noncombatants, ordinary folk. The hostility is generalized and indiscriminate. In the case of Islamic terrorism, the Enemy is the infidel, whose world leader is the United States and whose local representative is Israel.

Islamic terrorists don't call themselves freedom fighters; they have a different mission: to restore the dominance of Islam in the lands of Islam. Osama bin Laden, in the speech he delivered on video shortly before (it was broadcast after) the September 11 attacks, spoke about eighty years of subjection, which takes the story back to the establishment of European protectorates and trusteeships in the Middle East after World War I; the effort to create a Christian state in Lebanon; the effort to set up Western-style constitutional monarchies and parliamentary republics in the Arab world; the establishment of Israel as a Jewish state after the Second World War; and then the long series of military defeats from 1948 to 1991, not only in the Middle East but in East Asia, all of them experienced as terrible humiliations, at the hands of Jews, Hindus, and Americans, who are not supposed to be warrior peoples at all.

But the military defeats are part of a larger story of the failure of state building and economic development in most of the Islamic world. The fundamentalist religious response to modernity, which is common across all the major world religions, comes up here against governments that are very far from admirable representatives of modernity: secular governments often, or governments that are ready for accommodation with the West and eager to absorb the latest technologies, but at the same time brutal, repressive, corrupt, authoritarian, unjust . . . and unsuccessful in providing either the symbols or the substance of a decent common life. And some of these governments, in order to maintain their own power, sponsor a kind of ideological and theological scapegoating, directed against external enemies: Israel, America, the West generally, who are blamed for the internal failures. Some of these governments are our allies, Islamic moderates or Arab secularists, but they have yet to take on the extremists in their midst; they have yet to commit themselves to an open struggle against the theological radicalism that inspires the terrorist networks. Jihad is a response not only to modernity but also to the radical failure of the Islamic world to modernize itself.

Earlier terrorist campaigns are also explicable, in part, by the internal authoritarianism and weakness of the "liberation movement," in this case, its refusal or inability to mobilize its own people for other kinds of political action. Terrorism, after all, doesn't require mass mobilization; it is the work of a tiny elite of militants, who claim to represent "the people" but who act in the absence of the people (that's why classical Marxism was always hostile to terrorism — the reason, alas, was strategic, not moral). When someone like Gandhi was able to organize a nonviolent mass movement for national liberation, there was no terrorism.

3. *How is terrorism defended?* In certain extremist Islamic groups today there is a straightforward defense, which is also a denial: there are no innocent Americans, hence attacks like those of September 11 are not terrorist in character. But the arguments that I want to consider are of a different sort: they don't justify the acts that we call terrorism. Instead, they are expressions of what I have already described as a culture of excuse and apology. There are basically two kinds of excuses. The first looks to the desperation of the "oppressed," as they are called (and as they

may well be): terror, we are told, is the weapon of the weak, the last resort of subject nations. In fact, terror is commonly the first resort of militants who believe from the beginning that the Enemy should be killed and who are neither interested in nor capable of organizing their own people for any other kind of politics: the FLN and the PLO resorted to terror from the beginning; there was no long series of attempts to find alternatives. And as we have seen, there is at least one alternative—nonviolent mass mobilization—that has proven itself a far more effective "weapon of the weak."

The second kind of excuse looks to the guilt of the victims of terrorism. Here is how it works for Americans: we fought the Gulf War, we station troops on the sacred soil of Saudi Arabia, we blockade and bomb Iraq, we support Israel—what do we expect? Of course, the September 11 attacks were wrong; they ought to be condemned; but—a very big "but"—after all, we deserved it; we had it coming. Generally, this argument comes from people who before September 11 wanted us to stop protecting the Kurds in northern Iraq, to stop supporting Israel, and to get out of Saudi Arabia; and now they see a chance to use Islamic terrorism as a kind of "enforcer" for their own political agenda. They attribute their agenda to the terrorists (what else could terrorists have in mind but what Western leftists have always advocated?), and then call for a policy of appeasement in order to avoid further attacks. That is a policy, it seems to me, that would begin with dishonor and end in disaster. But I won't talk about that now; I want simply to deny the moral legitimacy of the excuse. Even if American policies in the Middle East and in East Asia have been or are wrong in many ways, they don't excuse the terrorist attack; they don't even make it morally comprehensible. The murder of innocent people is not excusable.

4. *How should we respond?* I want to argue for a multilateral response, a "war" against terror that has to be fought on many fronts. But who is the enemy here? Is it the people who planned or sponsored or supported the September 11 attacks or is it any and all other groups that practice a terrorist politics? I suggest that we think in terms of an analogy with humanitarian intervention. We (the United States, the United Nations, the North Atlantic Treaty Organization, the Organization of African Unity, and others) intervene, or ought to intervene, against genocide and "ethnic cleansing" wherever they occur. There are, of course, many different political and religious doctrines that inspire genocide and ethnic cleansing, and each intervention is distinct; each one requires its own calculations of morality and prudence. But our commitment should be general. The case is the same with terror: there are many terrorist ideologies and many terrorist organizations. We should oppose them all, but the different engagements will have to be considered one by one. We should imagine the "war" as including many possible engagements.

"War" is a metaphor here, but real war is a necessary part of the metaphorical "war." It may be the only part to which the frequently invoked doctrine of "just war" applies; we will have to look for other, though not unrelated, kinds of ethical guidance on the other fronts. The question about justice in the real war is a familiar one, and so is the answer — though the answer is easier in principle than in practice. In fighting against terrorists, we must not aim at innocent people (that's what the terrorists do); ideally we should get close enough to the enemy, or to his supporters, so that we are quite sure not only that we are aiming at them but also that we are hitting them. When we fight from far away, with planes and missiles, we have to get people in, on the ground, to select the targets, or we have to have very good intelligence; we must avoid overestimating the smartness of our smart bombs. Technological hubris isn't, I suppose, a crime, but it can lead to very bad outcomes, so it is better to leave a wide margin for error. And, finally, because even if we do all these things, we will still be imposing serious risks on the civilian population, we must reduce those risks as far as possible — and take risks ourselves in order to do that. This last is the hardest thing I have to say, because I'm not the one who will have to take those risks. The proportionality rule is commonly invoked here: civilian deaths and injuries, euphemistically called "collateral damage," should not be disproportionate to the value of the military victory that is being sought. But because I don't know how to measure the relevant values or how to specify the proportionality, and because I don't think that anyone else knows, I prefer to focus instead on the seriousness of the intention to avoid harming civilians, and that is best measured by the acceptance of risk.

Assuming that we correctly identified the terrorist network responsible for the September 11 attacks and that the Taliban government was in fact its patron and protector, the war in Afghanistan is certainly a just one. The point of the war is prevention above all: to destroy the network and stop the preparation of future attacks. We shouldn't, in my view, think of the war as a "police action," aimed at bringing criminals to justice. We probably don't have the evidence to do that; and it may well be the case that evidence collected by clandestine means or by armed force in distant countries, evidence that doesn't come from official archives, such as the German records that figured in the Nuremberg trials, but from e-mail intercepts and similar unofficial sources, would not be admissible in an American court — and probably not in international courts either, though I don't know what rules of evidence apply in The Hague. In any case, do we really want trials now, while the terrorist networks are still active? Think of the hostage-takings and bomb threats that would almost certainly accompany them. The use of military courts would avoid these difficulties, because the rules of evidence could be relaxed and the trials held in secret. But then there will be costs to pay in legitimacy: for justice, as the saying goes, must not only be done, it must be seen to be done; it must be seen *being* done. So . . . there may be trials down the road, but we shouldn't focus on them now; the first object of the "war" against terrorism is not backward looking and retributive, but forward looking and preventive. If that's the point, then there is a sense in which Afghanistan is a sideshow, however necessary it is, however much attention the media give it, however focused on it our diplomats and soldiers have to be.

The most important battle against terror is being waged right here, and in Britain and Germany and Spain, and other countries of the Arab and Islamic diaspora. If we can prevent further attacks, if we can begin to roll up the terrorist cells, that will be a major victory. And it is very, very important, because "successes" like September 11 have energizing effects; they produce a rush of recruits and probably a new willingness to fund the terrorist networks.

Police work is the first priority, and that raises questions, not about justice, but about civil liberties. Liberals and libertarians leap to the defense of liberty, and they are right to leap; but when they (we) do that, we have to accept a new burden of proof: we have to be able to make the case that the necessary police work can be done, and can be done effectively, within whatever constraints we think are required for the sake of American freedom. If we can't make that case, then we have to be ready to consider modifying the constraints. It isn't a betrayal of liberal or American values to do that; it is in fact the right thing to do, because the first obligation of the state is to protect the lives of its citizens (that's what states are for), and American lives are now visibly and certainly at risk. Again, prevention is crucial. Think of what will happen to our civil liberties if there are more successful terrorist attacks.

Covert action is also necessary, and I confess that I don't know what moral rules apply to it. The combatant-noncombatant distinction is crucial to every kind of political and military activity; beyond that it is hard to know. Moral argument requires its cases, and here the cases are, deliberately and presumably rightly, concealed from view. Perhaps I can say a word about assassination, which has been much discussed in recent months. The killing of political leaders is ruled out in international law, even (or especially) in wartime — and ruled out for good reason — because it is the political leaders of the enemy state with whom we will one day have to negotiate the peace. There are obvious exceptions to this rule — no one, no moral person, would have objected to an allied effort to assassinate Hitler; we were in fact not prepared to negotiate with him — but ordinary political leaders are immune. Diplomats are immune for the same reason: they are potential peacemakers. But military leaders are not immune, however high they stand on the chain of command. We have as much right to shell the enemy army's central headquarters as to shell its front-line positions. With terrorist organizations, this distinction between military and political leaders probably collapses; the two are hard to mark off, and we are not planning on negotiations. At any rate, it would seem odd to say that it is legitimate to attack a group of terrorists-in-training in a camp in Afghanistan, say, but not legitimate to go after the man who is planning the operation for which the others are training. That can't be right.

Diplomatic work comes next: right now it is focused on building support for military action in Afghanistan and for some kind of future non-Taliban regime. But over the long run, the critically important task will be to isolate and punish states that support terrorism. The networks look transnational; they exploit the globalist modernity that they so bitterly oppose. But make no mistake: neither the transnational networks, nor most of the more provincial ones, could survive without the physical shelter, the ideological patronage, and the funding provided by such states as Iran, Syria, Libya, and others. We are not going to go to war with those states; there is no *causus belli*, nor should we look for one. But there are many forms of legitimate political and economic pressure short of war, and it seems to me that we have to work hard to bring that kind of pressure to bear. This means that we have to persuade other countries — our allies in many cases, who have closer ties than we do with terrorist states and whose leaders have not been heroes in these matters — to bring pressure of their own to bear and to support disinvestment, embargo, and other sanctions when they are appropriate.

War, police work, covert action, and diplomacy: all these are tasks of the state. But there is also ideological work, which can't and shouldn't be directed or organized by the state, which will only be effective if it is carried on freely — and that means in the usual democratically haphazard and disorderly way. I suppose that the state can get involved, with the Voice of America and other media. But what I have in mind is different. Secular and religious intellectuals, scholars, preachers, and publicists, not necessarily in any organized way, but with some sense of shared commitment, have to set about delegitimizing the culture of excuse and apology, probing the religious and nationalist sources of terror, calling upon the best in Islamic civilization against the worst, defending the separation of religion and politics in all civilizations. This sort of thing is very important; argument is very important. It may sound self-serving for someone who makes his living making arguments to say this, but it is true nonetheless. For all their inner-directedness, their fanatical commitment and literal-minded faith, terrorists do rely on, and the terrorist organizations rely even more on, a friendly environment—and this friendly environment is a cultural/intellectual/ political creation. We have to work to transform the environment, so that wherever terrorists go, they will encounter hostility and rejection.

5. *What will be the signs of a successful response?* How will we know when we have won this "war"? We have already been told by the secretary of defense that we are not going to get the conventional signs: formal surrender, signatures on a peace treaty. The measure of success will be relative: a decline in attacks and in the scope of attacks; the collapse of morale among the terrorists, the appearance of informers and defectors from their ranks; the rallying of opportunists, who have the best nose for who's winning, to our side; the silence of those who once made excuses for terror; a growing sense of safety among ordinary people. None of this is going to come quickly or easily.

There is one more measure: our ability to shape our foreign policies, particularly toward the Islamic world, without worrying about the terrorist response. Right now, we have to worry: we cannot do things that would lead someone like bin Laden to claim a victory, to boast that he had forced our hand. We have to walk a fine line: to sustain a defensible policy with regard, say, to the blockade of Iraq, the Arab-Israeli conflict, and the Kashmir dispute, and not to do anything that can plausibly be construed as appeasement. [But see "Terrorism: A Critique of Excuses" (Chapter 4) for the necessary limits of this argument. It must not become an excuse for indefensible policies.] There are American policies (not only in the Islamic world, but globally as well) that should be changed, but in politics one must not only do the right thing, one must do it for the right reasons; the attacks of September 11 are not a good reason for change. One day we will be free of this kind of constraint, and that will be another way of knowing that we have won.

Inspectors Yes, War No
(September 2002)

The Bush administration is threatening to attack Iraq and has been doing so for many months now. But it is hard, even after the president's U.N. speech, to see the point of the threat. It might be intended to deter the Iraqis from developing weapons of mass destruction, but it seems more likely to speed up the work they are already doing — especially since George W. Bush has repeatedly insisted that his goal is not just to stop weapons development but also to overthrow the regime of Saddam Hussein. It might be intended to rally support for the war to come, but so far it has had exactly the opposite effect, giving every country in the world (and every former general in the U.S. Army) a chance to say no — a chance that many of them have eagerly seized. It might be intended to press Iraq to accept a renewed U.N. inspection system or to press our allies to impose such a system. That would be a rational goal, but it doesn't seem to be what the administration really wants. The United States has taken little part in the months-long negotiations aimed at bringing the inspectors back.

Without access to U.S. intelligence it is hard to judge how grave a threat Saddam poses. But let's make some commonsense stipulations: First, the Iraqis have developed chemical and biological weapons and are trying to develop nuclear weapons; second, our government isn't certain about how close they are to having a usable nuclear weapon, but as of this moment they don't have one; third, Iraq has used chemical weapons in the past, though only on its own territory during the war with Iran and in efforts to repress the Kurds; and fourth, the Iraqi regime is sufficiently brutal internally and hostile externally — to some of its neighbors and to the United States — that we can't rule out its readiness to use such weapons again and more widely or to use nuclear weapons if and when it develops them. We also can't rule out (though there is as yet no evidence for) the transfer of weapons of mass destruction from the Iraqi military or secret services to terrorist groups.

If these stipulations are plausible today, they have been plausible for a long time. They suggest how wrong it was to allow the first U.N. inspection system to collapse. There was a just and necessary war waiting to be fought back in the 1990s when Saddam was playing hide-and-seek with the inspectors. That would have been an internationalist war, a war of enforcement, and its justice would have derived, first, from the justice of the system it was enforcing and, second, from its likely outcome: the strengthening of the U.N. and the global legal order.

Though Iraq did not use weapons of mass destruction in the Gulf war, the peace agreement imposed after the war — which was authorized and, in part, implemented by the U.N. — included restrictions on the development and deployment of such weapons. As an aggressor state, Iraq was subjected to a set of constraints designed to make future aggression impossible. Imagine it as a state on parole, deprived of full sovereignty because of its previous behavior. This was a just outcome of the Gulf war, and the inspection system was its central feature.

Once the inspectors were in place, they revealed to the world how hard Saddam's government had been working on a variety of horrific weapons and how far along some of the work was. For a while, at least, the inspections seemed to be reasonably effective: A number of facilities and large quantities of dangerous materials were discovered and destroyed. But memory is short in political life, and commitments and coalitions are fragile. The urgencies of the war and its immediate aftermath receded, and some of Iraq's old trading partners, France and Russia most importantly, began to renew their ties. By the mid-'90s Saddam felt that he could safely test the will of the U.N. and the coalition of 1991, and so he began delaying the inspections or denying the inspectors access to the sites they wanted to visit. And he was right: There was no will to enforce the inspection system—not at the U.N. (which passed many resolutions but did nothing else), not in Europe, and not in the Clinton administration. The United States was prepared to use its airpower to maintain the "no-fly zones" in the North and South but was not prepared for a larger war.

If the inspectors had been forcibly supported, their employer, the U.N., would be much stronger than it currently is, and it would be very difficult for the United States or anyone else to plan a war without going through the U.N.'s decision-making procedures. But the failure of the '90s is not easy to rectify, and it doesn't help to pretend that the U.N. is an effective agent of global law and order when it isn't. Many states insist that they support the renewal of the inspection system, but so long as they are unwilling to use force on its behalf, their support is suspect. They profess to be defending the international rule of law, but how can the law "rule" when there is no law enforcement? When the Bush administration worries that the return of the inspectors would be (in Vice President Dick Cheney's words) "false comfort," it is reflecting a general belief, shared by Saddam, that our European allies would never agree to use force in order to ensure that those inspectors receive unfettered access to possible weapons-development sites. Indeed, until very recently, the Europeans were not seriously trying to renew the inspection system — probably because they were reluctant to face the enforcement question. U.N. negotiators dithered with Iraqi negotiators in a diplomatic dance that seems to have been designed for delay and ultimate failure. It still isn't clear that the dance is over.

Delay is dangerous because once Saddam has weapons of mass destruction and effective delivery systems, our threat to use force against Iraq will be far less plausible than it could be today. But as I have stipulated, Saddam doesn't have them yet. If the administration thinks that Iraq is already a nuclear power, or is literally on the verge of becoming one, then the past months of threatening war rather than fighting it would seem to represent, from the administration's perspective, something like criminal negligence. If there is even a little time before Iraq gets the bomb, the rapid restoration of the inspection system is surely the right thing to aim at — and immensely preferable to the "preemptive" war that many in Washington so eagerly support.

In a speech at West Point a few months ago, President Bush made a case for the necessity and justice of preemptive war against Iraq. But in the absence of evidence suggesting not only the existence of Iraqi weapons but also their imminent use, preemption is not an accurate description of what the president is threatening. No one expects an Iraqi attack tomorrow or next Tuesday, so there is nothing to preempt. The war that is being discussed is *preventive*, not preemptive — it is designed to respond to a more distant threat. The general argument for preventive war is very old; in its classic form it has to do with the balance of power. "Right now," says the prime minister of country X, "the balance is stable; each of the competing states feels that its power is sufficient to deter the others from attacking. But country Y, our historic rival across the river, is actively and urgently at work developing new weapons, preparing a mass mobilization; and if this work is allowed to continue, the balance will shift, and our deterrent power will no longer be effective. The only solution is to attack now, while we still can." International lawyers and just-war theorists have never looked on this argument with favor because the danger to which it alludes is not only distant but speculative, whereas the costs of a preventive war are near, certain, and usually terrible. The distant dangers, after all, might be avoided by diplomacy, or the military work of the other side might be matched by work on this side, or country X might look for alliances with states possessing the deterrent power that it lacks. Whether or not war is properly the last resort, there seems no sufficient reason for making it the first.

But the old argument for preventive war did not take into account weapons of mass destruction or delivery systems that allow no time for arguments about how to respond. Perhaps the gulf between preemption and prevention has now narrowed so that there is little strategic (and therefore little moral) difference between them. The Israeli attack on the Iraqi nuclear reactor in 1981 is sometimes invoked as an example of a justified preventive attack that was also, in a sense, preemptive: The Iraqi threat was not imminent, but an immediate attack was the only reasonable action against it. Once the reactor was in operation, an attack would have endangered civilians living many miles around it. So it was a question of now or never. A single attack could be effective now but not later; afterward, only a full-scale war could have prevented the Iraqi acquisition of nuclear weapons. But if this limited argument for preventive war applied to Israel in 1981, it does not apply to the United States in 2002. Iraq, after all, was already formally at war with Israel, and its hostility was visible, threatening, and immediate. Listening these days to Saddam's speeches, one might conclude that Israel still has a case for a preventive attack against Iraqi targets, and some of Iraq's other neighbors may also have a case: At least they confront a real threat. But I don't think that there is an American case, even if we claim to represent the neighbors — who have not authorized our representation and whose citizens would be radically at risk in any American war. In fact, the "now or never" example strengthens the argument for inspection. The first U.N. inspectors supervised the destruction of facilities and materials that would have been dangerous to bomb from the air; there is still time for them to do that again.

The administration's response, so far as I can make it out, has two parts. First, the inspectors will never get into Iraq, or will never be able to work effectively once they are in, unless there is a readiness to fight — and no one at the U.N. or in Europe is seriously ready. Inspection means delay, and again, delay is dangerous. Better to fight now. But "now" seems to be a fairly elastic term; clearly there are people in the Bush administration who think that the delays of the last months, and the likely delays of the coming months, are not so terribly dangerous. And the inspectors could probably be at work "now," in the more precise sense of that word, had there been a will to send them back.

Second, however effective they were, the inspectors would not overthrow the regime of Saddam Hussein. That sounds right, though their presence and their work would certainly weaken the regime. In any case, change of regime is not commonly accepted as a justification for war. The precedents are not encouraging: Guatemala, the Dominican Republic, Chile, Hungary, and Czechoslovakia all reflect the bad old days of cold war "spheres of influence" and ideologically driven military or clandestine interventions. Regime change can sometimes be the *consequence* of a just war—when the defeated rulers are moral monsters, like the Nazis in World War II. And humanitarian interventions to stop massacre and ethnic cleansing can also legitimately result in the installation of a new regime. But now that a zone of (relative) safety has been carved out for the Kurds in the North, there is no compelling case to be made for humanitarian intervention in Iraq. The Baghdad regime is brutally repressive and morally repugnant, certainly, but it is not engaged in mass murder or ethnic cleansing; there are governments as bad (well, almost as bad) all over the world.

The only compelling reason for targeting Saddam is the belief that he will never give up the pursuit of weapons of mass destruction. But even this is not persuasive. Faced with a unified international community committed to the enforcement of an inspections regime, with soldiers ready to move, Saddam would almost certainly suspend his pursuit—and the suspension would last as long as the commitment did. In any case, many other regimes around the world, including democratic regimes (such as India's), have developed or are trying to develop such weapons, so how can we be sure that future Iraqi rulers would not resume Saddam's project? If we are interested in the safety of Iraq's neighbors, inspection is a more reliable solution than regime change.

The right thing to do, right now, is to re-create the conditions that existed in the mid-'90s for fighting a just war. And we must do this precisely to avoid the war that many in the Bush administration want to fight. The Europeans could have reestablished these conditions by themselves months ago if they really wanted to challenge American unilateralism. No government in Baghdad could have resisted a European ultimatum—admit the inspectors by a certain date or else!—so long as the states behind the ultimatum included France and Russia, who have been Iraq's protectors, and so long as the "or else!" involved both economic and military action. Why didn't the Europeans do this? Bush spoke about a "difficult and defining moment" for the U.N., but it is really the Europeans who are being tested at this moment. So far, their conduct suggests that they have lost all sense of themselves as independent and responsible actors in international society. In an interview published in *The New York Times* on September 5, German Prime Minister Gerhard Schroeder made the amazing statement that when the U.S. government threatened war, it effectively blocked any effort to restore the inspection system. I am afraid that the truth is the exact opposite: There would be no effort at all without the threat. Four days after Schroeder's statement, in the *Times* again, French President Jacques Chirac called for the U.N. to reimpose the inspection system and to consider authorizing the use of force against Iraq if the inspectors were hindered in their work. It would have been a powerful sign of French independence had he said this to *Le Monde* in June or July. Now Chirac's proposal has to be viewed as nothing more than a last-minute effort to accommodate the crazy Americans. Still, the French proposal should be pursued. It has already helped to produce the Iraqi offer to readmit the inspectors. Chirac should now be challenged to insist on unfettered inspections even if Iraq begins introducing new caveats.

Convinced that France, Russia, and other European states (Great Britain being the only exception) are bent on appeasement, the United States hasn't moved on its own to restore the inspection system. But that is what we should do. Together, Europe and the United States could certainly impose the system that is needed, with the inspectors free to go wherever they want, on their own time schedule. This is a way to avoid, or at least to postpone, the war with Iraq. Let the inspectors go to work, but don't repeat the mistakes of the '90s; back them up with visible and overwhelming force.

I can't say right now if there is a good chance of getting the inspectors back. There are a lot of people eager to repeat the old mistakes. The real and only argument for war is not that war is the right choice, or the best available choice, but that there is no international commitment to actions short of war that require the *threat* of war. I think it is fair to say that many influential Europeans, from both the political class and the intelligentsia, would prefer a unilateral American war to a European readiness to fight — even if, as Hamlet says, "the readiness is all," and war itself could be avoided.

So we may yet face the hardest political question: What ought to be done when what ought to be done is not going to be done? But we shouldn't be too quick to answer that question. If the dithering and delay go on and on — if the inspectors don't return or if they return but can't work effectively; if the threat of enforcement is not made credible; and if our allies are unwilling to act — then many of us will probably end up, very reluctantly, supporting the war the Bush administration seems so eager to fight. Right now, however, there are other things to do, and there is still time to do them. The administration's war is neither just nor necessary.

The Right Way
(January 2003)

There are two ways of opposing a war with Iraq. The first way is simple and wrong; the second way is right but difficult.

The first way is to deny that the Iraqi regime is particularly ugly, that it lies somewhere outside the range of ordinary states, or to argue that, however ugly it is, it doesn't pose any significant threat to its neighbors or to world peace. Perhaps, despite Saddam's denials, his government is in fact seeking to acquire nuclear weapons. But other governments are doing the same thing, and if or when Iraq succeeds in developing such weapons — so the argument continues — we can deal with that through conventional deterrence, in exactly the same way that the United States and the Soviet Union dealt with each other in the Cold War years.

Obviously if this argument is right, there is no reason to attack Iraq. Nor is there any reason for a strong inspection system, or for the current embargo, or for the northern and southern "no-fly" zones. Some of the most vocal organizers of the antiwar movement, here and in Europe, seem to have adopted exactly this position. It has been overrepresented among speakers at the big demonstrations against the war. Most of the demonstrators, I believe, don't hold this first view; nor is it held by the wider constituency of actual and potential opponents of Bush's foreign policy. But we have to recognize a constant temptation of antiwar politics: to pretend that there really isn't a serious enemy out there.

This pretense certainly keeps things simple, but it is wrong in every possible way. The tyranny and brutality of the Iraqi regime are widely known and cannot be covered up. Its use of chemical weapons in the recent past; the recklessness of its invasions of Iran and Kuwait; the rhetoric of threat and violence that is now standard in Baghdad; the record of the 1990s, when U.N. inspectors were systematically obstructed; the cruel repression of the uprisings that followed the Gulf War of 1991; the torture and murder of political opponents — how can all this be ignored by a serious political movement? Nor should anyone be comfortable with the idea of an Iraq armed with nuclear weapons and then deterred from using them. Not only is it unclear that deterrence will work with a regime like Saddam's, but the emerging system of deterrence will be highly unstable. For it won't only involve the United States and Iraq; it will also involve Israel and Iraq. If Iraq is permitted to build nuclear weapons, Israel will have to acquire what it doesn't have at the present time: second-strike capacity. And then there will be Israeli ships in the Mediterranean Sea and the Indian Ocean equipped with nuclear weapons on hair-trigger alert. This may be "conventional" deterrence, but it is insane to look forward to it.

The right way to oppose the war is to argue that the present system of containment and control is working and can be made to work better. This means that we should acknowledge the awfulness of the Iraqi regime and the dangers it poses and then aim to deal with those dangers through coercive measures short of war. But this isn't a policy easy to defend, for we know exactly what coercive measures are necessary, and we also know how costly they are.

First, the existing embargo: this can and should be adjusted to allow into the country a wider range of products necessary to the civilian population while still excluding military supplies and the technologies necessary to the development of weapons of mass destruction. But however "smart" the sanctions are, they will still constitute a partial blockade and a forceful restraint of trade, and, given the way Saddam spends his available funds, they will impose severe hardships on ordinary Iraqis. It is fair to say that their own government is responsible for these hardships, since it could spend its money differently, but that does not make them easier to bear. Malnourished children, hospitals without medical supplies, declining longevity rates: all these are the (indirect) consequence of the embargo.

Second, the no-fly zones: preventing Iraqi planes from flying over an area that amounts to about half of the country requires constant American overflights, and this requires in turn what has averaged out as twice-weekly bombings of radar and antiaircraft facilities. So far, no planes or pilots have been lost, and I believe that few civilians have been killed or injured in the bombing raids. Still, this is a risky and costly business, and if it is short of war, it isn't far short. On the other hand, if Saddam were allowed free rein in the north and south, against the Kurds and the Shi'ites, the result would probably be a repression so brutal that it would justify, perhaps even require, a military intervention on humanitarian grounds. And that would be a full-scale war.

Third, the U.N. inspections: these will have to go on indefinitely, as a regular feature of the Iraqi landscape. For whether or not the inspectors find and destroy weapons of mass destruction (some of these are very easy to hide), they themselves are a barrier to any deployment of such weapons. So long as they are moving freely and aggressively around the country, on their own time schedule, Iraq will be under increasing restraint. But the inspection regime will collapse, as it collapsed in the 1990s, unless there is a visible readiness to use force to sustain it. And this means that there have to be troops in the vicinity, like the troops the U.S. government is currently moving into position. It would be better, obviously, if these troops were not only American. But, again, maintaining a readiness of this sort, whoever maintains it, is costly and risky.

Defending the embargo, the American overflights, and the U.N. inspections: this is the right way to oppose, and to avoid, a war. But it invites the counterargument that a short war — which would make it possible to end the embargo, and the weekly bombings, and the inspection regime — would be morally and politically preferable to this "avoidance." A short war, a new regime, a demilitarized Iraq, food and medicine pouring into Iraqi ports: wouldn't that be better than a permanent system of coercion and control? Well, maybe. But who can guarantee that the war would be short and that the consequences in the region and elsewhere would be limited?

We say of war that it is the "last resort" because of the unpredictable, unexpected, unintended, and unavoidable horrors that it regularly brings. In fact, war isn't the last resort, for "lastness" is a metaphysical condition, which is never actually reached in real life: it is always possible to do something else, or to do it again, before doing whatever it is that comes last. The notion of lastness is cautionary — but this caution is necessary: look hard for alternatives before you "let loose the dogs of war."

Right now, even at this last minute, there still are alternatives, and that is the best argument against going to war. I think it is a widely accepted argument, even though it isn't easy to march with. What do you write on the placards? What slogans do you shout? We need a complicated campaign against the war, whose participants are ready to acknowledge the difficulties and the costs of their politics.

Or, better, we need a campaign that isn't focused only on the war (and that might survive the war) — a campaign for a strong international system, organized and designed to defeat aggression, to stop massacres and ethnic cleansing, to control weapons of mass destruction, and to guarantee the physical security of all the world's peoples. The threefold constraints on Saddam's regime are only one example, but a very important one, of how such an international system should function.

But an international system has to be the work of many different states, not of one state. There have to be many agents ready to take responsibility for the success of the system, not just one. Today, the U.N. inspection regime is in place in Iraq only because of what many American liberals and leftists, and many Europeans too, called a reckless U.S. threat to go to war. Without that threat, however, U.N. negotiators would still be dithering with Iraqi negotiators, working on, but never finally agreeing on, the details of an inspection system; the inspectors would not even have packed their bags (and most of the leaders of Europe would be pretending that this was a good thing). Some of us are embarrassed to realize that the threat we opposed is the chief reason for the existence of a strong inspection system, and the existence of a strong inspection system is today the best argument against going to war.

It would have been much better if the U.S. threat had not been necessary — if the threat had come, say, from France and Russia, Iraq's chief trading partners, whose unwillingness to confront Saddam and give some muscle to the U.N. project was an important cause of the collapse of inspections in the 1990s. This is what internationalism requires: that other states besides the United States take responsibility for the global rule of law and that they be prepared to act, politically and militarily, with that end in view.

American internationalists — there are a good number of us, though not enough — need to criticize the Bush administration's unilateralist impulses and its refusal to cooperate with other states on a whole range of issues, from global warming to the International Criminal Court. But multilateralism requires help from outside the United States. It would be easier to make our case if it were clear that there were other agents in international society capable of acting independently and, if necessary, forcefully, and ready to answer for what they do, in places like Bosnia, or Rwanda, or Iraq. When we campaign against a second Gulf War, we should also be campaigning for that kind of multilateral responsibility. And this means that we have demands to make not only on Bush and Co. but also on the leaders of France and Germany, Russia and China, who, although they have recently been supporting continued and expanded inspections, have also been ready, at different times in the past, to appease Saddam. If this preventable war is fought, all of them will share responsibility with the United States. When the war is over, they should all be held to account.

What a Little War Could Do
(March 2003)

The United States is marching to war as if there were no alternative. Judging from President Bush's press conference last night [March 6], the administration seems to have no exit strategy, no contingency plans to stop the march. Our leaders have created a situation where any failure to fight would count as a victory for Saddam Hussein and Jacques Chirac.

Would that victory be worse than the war itself? It could be, if it served only to postpone the war. The French would claim to have saved the peace; Saddam Hussein would claim to have defeated the American effort to overthrow him. But then, down the road, the United States would almost certainly have to fight under harder conditions against a stronger Iraq.

The American march is depressing, but the failure of opponents of the war to offer a plausible alternative is equally depressing. France and Russia undoubtedly raised the diplomatic stakes on Wednesday by threatening to veto a new Security Council resolution authorizing the use of force in Iraq. But they once again failed to follow up the rhetoric with anything meaningful.

What would a plausible alternative look like? The way to avoid a big war is to intensify the little war that the United States is already fighting. It is using force against Iraq every day — to protect the no-fly zones and to stop and search ships heading for Iraqi ports. Only the American threat to use force makes the inspections possible — and possibly effective.

When the French claim that force is a "last resort," they are denying that the little war is going on. And, indeed, France is not participating in it in any significant way. The little war is almost entirely the work of American and British forces; the opponents of the big war have not been prepared to join or support or even acknowledge the work that the little war requires.

But Mr. Bush could stop the American march toward the big war if he challenged the French (and the Germans and the Russians) to join the little war. The result would not be a victory for Mr. Hussein or Mr. Chirac, and it would ensure that the Iraqi regime would get weaker over time.

So here is an exit strategy for the Bush administration. They haven't asked for it, but they need it. First, extend the northern and southern no-fly zones to include the whole country. America has already drastically restricted Iraqi sovereignty, so this would not be anything new. There are military reasons for the extension — the range of missiles, the speed of planes, the reach of radar all make it difficult for the United States and Britain to defend the northern and the southern regions of Iraq without control of central airspace. But the main reason would be punitive: Iraq has never accepted the containment regime put in place after the Gulf War, and its refusal to do that should lead to tighter and tighter containment.

Second, impose the "smart sanctions" that the Bush administration talked about before 9/11 and insist that Iraq's trading partners commit themselves to enforcing them. Washington should announce sanctions of its own against countries that don't cooperate, and it should also punish any companies that try to sell military equipment to Iraq.

Third, the United States should expand the U.N. monitoring system in all the ways that have recently been proposed: adding inspectors, bringing in U.N. soldiers (to guard military installations after they have been inspected), sending surveillance planes without providing forty-eight hours' notice, and so on.

Finally, the United States should challenge the French to make good on their claim that force is indeed a last resort by mobilizing troops of their own and sending them to the gulf. Otherwise, what they are saying is that if things get very bad, they will unleash the American army. And Saddam Hussein knows that the French will never admit that things have gotten that bad. So, if they are serious, the French have to mount a credible threat of their own. Or, better, they have to join the United States in every aspect of the little war.

If an American proposal along these lines received strong international support, if there were a real commitment to sustain the little war for as long as necessary, there would be no good reason for the big war. The march could safely be stopped.

So, Is This a Just War?
(March 2003)

So, is this a just war? The question is of a very specific kind. It doesn't ask whether the war is legitimate under international law or whether it is politically or militarily prudent to fight it now (or ever). It asks only if it is morally defensible: just or unjust? I leave law and strategy to other people.

Saddam's war is unjust, even though he didn't start the fighting. He is not defending his country against a conquering army; he is defending his regime, which, given its record of aggression abroad and brutal repression at home, has no moral legitimacy; and he is resisting the disarmament of his regime, which was ordered (though not enforced) by the United Nations. This is a war that he could have avoided simply by meeting the demands of the U.N. inspectors — or, at the end, by accepting exile for the good of his country. Admittedly, self-defense is the paradigmatic case of just war, but the self in question is supposed to be a collective self, not a single person or a tyrannical clique seeking desperately to hold on to power, at whatever cost to ordinary people.

America's war is unjust. Though disarming Iraq is a legitimate goal, morally and politically, it is a goal that we could almost certainly have achieved with measures short of full-scale war. I have always resisted the argument that force is a last resort, because the idea of lastness is often, as the French demonstrated this past fall and winter, merely an excuse for postponing the use of force indefinitely. But force was necessary to every aspect of the containment regime that was the only real alternative to war — and it was necessary from the beginning. Force is not a matter of all or nothing, and it isn't a matter of first or last (or now or never): its use must be timely and proportional. At this

time, the threat that Iraq posed could have been met with something less than the war we are now fighting. And a war fought
before its time is not a just war.

But now that we are fighting it, I hope that we win it and that
the Iraqi regime collapses quickly. I will not march to stop the
war while Saddam is still standing, for that would strengthen his
tyranny at home and make him, once again, a threat to all his
neighbors. My argument with the antiwar demonstrators hangs
on the relative justice of two possible endings: either an American victory or anything short of that, which Saddam could call
a victory for himself. But, some of the demonstrators will ask,
wouldn't the first of these vindicate the disastrous diplomacy of
the Bush administration that led up to the war? Yes, it might do
that, but, on the other hand, the second ending would vindicate
the equally disastrous diplomacy of the French, who rejected
every opportunity to provide an alternative to war. And, again, it
would strengthen Saddam's hand.

But even people who were against starting the war can still
insist that it should be fought in accordance with the two crucial
commitments undertaken by the Bush administration. First, that
everything possible be done to avoid or reduce civilian casualties:
this is the central requirement of *jus in bello*, "justice in the conduct of war," which all armies in all wars are obligated to meet,
whatever the moral status of the war itself. Second, that everything possible be done to ensure that the post-Saddam regime be
a government of, by, and for the Iraqi people: this is the central
requirement of what might be called *jus post bellum* — the least
developed part of just war theory but obviously important these
days. Democracy may be a utopian aspiration, given the history
of Iraq and the foreign-policy record of the United States in
the past half-century; it certainly isn't easy to imagine realizing

it. But something better than the Baath in Baghdad is easy to imagine, and we are morally bound to seek a political arrangement that accommodates the Kurds and the Shi'ites, whatever difficulties that involves.

The critique of American unilateralism should focus for now on the effort to achieve a just ending for this second gulf war. And so should the critique of European irresponsibility. The United States will need help in Iraq (as we needed and still need help in Afghanistan), and that immediately raises two questions: Are we willing to ask other countries, or the United Nations as their representative, to play a significant role in the political and economic reconstruction of Iraq? And are France, Germany, and Russia ready to play such a role, which means to take responsibility, along with us, for a decent outcome? Those three countries were not willing to take responsibility for a serious containment regime before the war; nor were we willing to invite their participation in a regime of that sort. We were committed, too soon, to war; they were committed, all along, to appeasement. A cooperative effort to bring political decency to Iraq, and to help rebuild the country's economy, might begin to create the middle ground where multilateralism could take root.

And then we can go to work on the Bush administration's environmental record, and its opposition to the International Criminal Court, and its cancellation of the test ban treaty, and its claim to a hegemonic power beyond challenge, and . . .

Just and Unjust Occupations
(November 2003)

How is postwar justice related to the justice of the war itself and the conduct of its battles? Iraq poses this question in an especially urgent way, but the question would be compelling even without Iraq. It seems clear that you can fight a just war, and fight it justly, and still make a moral mess of the aftermath — by establishing a satellite regime, for example, or by seeking revenge against the citizens of the defeated (aggressor) state, or by failing, after a humanitarian intervention, to help the people you have rescued to rebuild their lives. But is the opposite case also possible: to fight an unjust war and then produce a decent postwar political order? That possibility is harder to imagine, since wars of conquest are unjust *ad bellum* and *post bellum*, before and after, and so, presumably, are wars of economic aggrandizement. These two are acts of theft — of sovereignty, territory, or resources — and so they end with critically important goods in the wrong hands. But a misguided military intervention or a preventive war fought before its time might nonetheless end with the displacement of a brutal regime and the construction of a decent one. Or a war unjust on both sides might result in a settlement, negotiated or imposed, that is fair to both and makes for a stable peace between them. I doubt that a settlement of this sort would retrospectively justify the war (in the second case, whose war would it justify?), but it might still be just in itself.

If this argument is right, then we need criteria for *jus post bellum* that are distinct from (though not wholly independent of) those that we use to judge the war and its conduct. We have to be able to argue about aftermaths as if this were a new argument — because, though it often isn't, it might be. The Iraq war is a case in point. The American debate about whether to fight doesn't seem particularly relevant to the critical issues in the debate about the occupation: how long to stay, how much to spend, when to begin the transfer of power — and, finally, who should answer these questions. The positions we took before the war don't determine the positions we take, or should take, on the occupation. Some people who opposed the war demand that we immediately "bring the troops home." But others argue, rightly, it seems to me, that having fought the war, we are now responsible for the well-being of the Iraqi people; we have to provide the resources — soldiers and dollars — necessary to guarantee their security and begin the political and economic reconstruction of their country. Still others argue that the aftermath of the war has to be managed by international agencies like the U.N. Security Council, with contributions from many countries that were not part of the war at all. And then the leaders of those countries ask, Why are we responsible for its costs?

Whatever one thinks about these different views, debating them requires an account of postwar justice. Democratic political theory, which plays a relatively small part in our arguments about *jus ad bellum* and *in bello*, provides the central principles of this account. They include self-determination, popular legitimacy, civil rights, and the idea of a common good. We want wars to end with governments in power in the defeated states that are chosen by the people they rule — or at least recognized by them as legitimate — and that are visibly committed to the welfare of those same people (all of them). We want minorities protected against persecution, neighboring states protected against aggression, the poorest of the people protected against destitution and starvation. In Iraq, we have (officially) set our sights even higher than this, on a fully democratic and federalist Iraq, but postwar justice is probably best understood in a minimalist way. It is not as if victors in war have been all that successful at achieving the minimum.

The timetable for self-determination depends heavily on the

character of the previous regime and the extent of its defeat. After the defeat of Germany in World War II, there was a four-year military occupation, during which many Nazi leaders were brought to trial and a general "denazification" was instituted. I don't believe that any of the Allied powers called for an early transfer of sovereignty to the German people. It was widely accepted that the neighboring states and all the internal and external victims of Nazism had this entitlement: that the new German regime be definitively post-Nazi. We can argue for a much quicker transfer of power in Iraq, since a large majority of the population, Kurds in the north and Shi'ites in the south, were not complicit in Baathist tyranny, which seems to have had a narrowly regional and sectarian base. But the tyrannical regime is still being defended from that base, which means that "debaathification" is still a necessary political-military process, so that Iraqis participating in (what we hope will be) an open society, forming civil associations, joining parties and movements, don't do so in fear of a restoration.

We don't seem to have thought much about this process in advance of the war or to have carried it out, thus far, with anything like the necessary understanding of Iraqi politics or history. What is the relation of planned and unplanned occupations to just and unjust occupations? Surely occupying powers are morally bound to think seriously about what they are going to do in someone else's country. That moral test we have obviously failed to meet.

But what determines the overall justice of a military occupation is less its planning or its length than its political direction and the distribution of the benefits it provides. If its steady tendency is to empower the locals and if its benefits are widely distributed, the occupying power can plausibly be called just. If power is tightly held and the procedures and motives of decision-making are concealed, if resources accumulated for the occupation end up in the hands of foreign companies and local favorites, then the occupation is unjust. Postbellum judgments are probably easier to make than those we are forced to make in the heat of battle; still, I want to make them explicit.

A just occupation costs money; it doesn't make money. Of course, the occupying army, like every army, will attract camp followers; these are the scavengers of war, profiteering at the margins. In the Iraqi case, however, President Bush and his advisers seem committed to profiteering at the center. They claim to be bringing democracy to Iraq, and we all have to hope that they succeed. But with much greater speed and effectiveness, they have brought to Iraq the crony capitalism that now prevails in Washington. And this undercuts the legitimacy of the occupation and puts its putative democratic goals in jeopardy.

The distribution of contracts to politically connected American companies is a scandal. But would it make any difference if the United Nations were distributing contracts to politically connected French, German, or Russian companies? In both cases, there has to be someone regulating the conduct of the companies — not only their honesty and efficiency but also their readiness to employ, and gradually yield authority to, competent Iraqi managers and technicians. An international agency of proven impartiality would be best, but even American regulators, under congressional mandate, would be an improvement over no regulators at all. The combination of unilateralism and laissez-faire is a recipe for disaster.

A multilateral occupation would be better than the unilateralist regime we have established — for legitimacy, certainly, and probably for efficiency — but at this writing that does not seem a lively prospect. It is easy and right to argue for an authoritative role for the U.N., but the argument is plausible only if the U.N. can mobilize the resources to take charge of Iraq as it is today. The countries that would have to provide the resources insist, however, that since this was an American war, America must bear the costs of the occupation — and also of political and economic reconstruction. This was a war of choice, they say, politically and morally unnecessary, and what one chooses in such a case is the whole thing: the war and its aftermath, with all their attendant burdens. It's a strong argument; many critics of the war made it even before the fighting began. *Jus post bellum* can't be entirely independent of *jus ad bellum*. The distribution of the costs of the settlement is necessarily related to the moral character of the war. But there is still a case to be made for the partial independence of the two and then for a wider distribution of the burdens of Iraq's reconstruction.

Whatever the prehistory of its achievement, a stable and democratic Iraq, even a relatively stable and more or less democratic Iraq, would be a good thing for the Middle East generally, for Europe and Japan, and (if it was involved in the achievement) for the United Nations. Given the likely benefits, why shouldn't the international community contribute to the costs of an occupation whose justice it could then guarantee? If the European Union had a larger sense of its global responsibilities, if its constituent states were really interested in modifying American behavior (rather than just complaining about it), they would make the contribution. But that is not going to happen. The Europeans want to share authority without sharing costs; the Bush administration wants to share costs without sharing authority. It is possible to imagine a makeshift compromise between them but

not a serious cooperation. These are opposed but equally unten-
able positions, and the result of the opposition is simply to con-
firm American unilateralism.

So the justice of the occupation is up to the citizens of the
United States. Here are the tests that the Bush administration
has to meet, and that we should insist on: first, the administration
must be prepared to spend the money necessary for reconstruction; second, it must be committed to debaathification and to the
equal protection of Iraq's different ethnic and religious groups;
third, it must be prepared to cede power to a legitimate and
genuinely independent Iraqi government — which could even, if
the bidding went that way, give its oil contracts to European
rather than American companies.

It sometimes turns out that occupying is harder than fighting.

PART THREE
futures

Imagine the possible political arrangements of international society as if they were laid out along a continuum marked off according to the degree of centralization. Obviously, there are alternative markings; the recognition and enforcement of human rights could also be measured along a continuum, as could democratization, welfare provision, pluralism, and so on. But focusing on centralization is the quickest way to reach the key political and moral questions, above all the classical question: what is the best or the best possible regime? What constitutional goals should we set ourselves in an age of globalization?

My plan is to present seven possible regimes or constitutions or political arrangements. I will do this discursively, without providing a list in advance, but I do want to list the criteria against which the seven arrangements have to be evaluated: these are their capacity to promote peace, distributive justice, cultural pluralism, and individual freedom. Within the scope of this essay, I will have to deal summarily with some of the arrangements and some of the criteria. Because the criteria turn out to be inconsistent with—or at least in tension with—one another, my argument will be complicated, but it could be, and no doubt should be, much more so.

It's best to begin with the two ends of the continuum, so that its dimensions are immediately visible. On one side, let's say the left side (though I will raise some doubts about that designation later on), there is a unified global state, something like Immanuel Kant's "world republic," with a single set of citizens, identical with the set of adult human beings, all of them possessed of the same rights and obligations. This is the form that maximum centralization would take: each individual, every person in the world, would be connected directly to the center. A global empire, in which one nation ruled over all the others, would also operate from a single center, but insofar as its rulers differentiated between the dominant nation and all the others, and perhaps among the others too, this would represent a qualification on its centralized character. The centralization of the global state, by contrast, is unqualified. Following Thomas Hobbes's argument in *Leviathan*, I want to say that such a state could be a monarchy, oligarchy, or democracy; its unity is not affected by its political character. By contrast, unity is certainly affected by any racial, religious, or ethnic divisions, whether these are hierarchical in nature, as in the imperial case, establishing significant inequalities among the groups, or merely functional or regional. Any political realization of difference moves us rightward on the continuum as I am imagining it.

At the far right is the regime or the absence-of-regime that political theorists call "international anarchy." This phrase describes what is in fact a highly organized world, but one that is radically decentered. The organizations are individual sovereign states, and there is no effective law binding on all of them. There is no global authority or procedure for policy determination and no encompassing legal jurisdiction for either sovereigns or citizens. More than this (since I mean to describe an extreme condition), there are no smaller groups of states that have accepted a common law and submitted to its enforcement by international agencies; there are no stable organizations of states working to generate common policies with regard, say, to environmental questions, arms control, labor standards, the movement of capital, or any other issue of general concern. Sovereign states negotiate with each other on the basis of their "national interests," reach agreements, and sign treaties, but the treaties are not enforceable by any third party. State leaders watch each other nervously and respond to each other's policies, but in every other sense, the centers of political decision making are independent; every state acts alone. This is not an account of our own situation; I am not describing the world as it is in 2000. But we are obviously closer to the right than to the left side of the continuum.

The strategy of this essay will be to move in from the two sides. I will be moving toward the center, but from opposite directions, so as to make clear that I am not describing a developmental or progressive history. The different regimes or arrangements are ideal types, not historical examples. And I don't assume in advance that the best regime lies at the center, only that it doesn't lie at the extremes. Even that assumption needs to be justified; so I had better turn immediately to the twin questions: What's wrong with radical centralization? What's wrong with anarchy? The second of these is the easier, because it is closer to our own experience. Anarchy leads regularly to war—and war to conquest, conquest to empire, empire to oppression, oppression to rebellion and secession, and secession leads back to anarchy and war again. The viciousness of the circle is continually reinforced by inequalities of wealth and power among the involved states and by the shifting character of these inequalities (which depend on trade patterns, technological development, military alliances, and so on). All this makes for insecurity and fear not only among the rulers of states but also among their ordinary inhabitants, and insecurity and fear are, as Hobbes argued, the chief cause of war.

But would an international society, however anarchic, all of whose constituent states were republics, be drawn into the same circle? Kant argued that republican citizens would be far less willing to accept the risks of war than kings were to impose those risks on their subjects — and so would be less threatening to their neighbors (*Perpetual Peace*, First Definitive Article). We certainly see evidence of that unwillingness in contemporary democracies, though it has not always been as strong as it is today. At the same time, it is qualified today by the willing use of the most advanced military technologies — which don't, indeed, put their users at risk though they impose very high costs on their targets. So it may be the case, as the Kosovo war suggests, that modern democracies won't live up to Kant's pacific expectations: they will fight, only not on the ground.

A rather different argument has been made by some contemporary political scientists: at least in modern times, democratic republics don't fight *with one another*. But if this is so, it is in part because they have had common enemies and have established multilateral forms of cooperation and coordination, alliances for mutual security, that mitigate the anarchy of their relations. They have moved, so to speak, to the left along the continuum.

But I don't want to dismiss international anarchy without saying something about its advantages. Despite the hazards of inequality and war, sovereign statehood is a way of protecting distinct historical cultures, sometimes national, sometimes ethnic/religious in character. The passion with which stateless nations pursue statehood and the driven character of national liberation movements reflect the somber realities of the twentieth century, from which it is necessary to draw moral and political conclusions for the twenty-first. Sovereign power is a means of self-protection, and it is very dangerous to be deprived of this means. So, the *morally* maximal form of decentralization would be a global society in which every national or ethnic/religious group that needed protection actually possessed sovereign power. But for reasons we all know, which have to do with the necessary territorial extension of sovereignty, the mix of populations on the ground, and the uneven distribution of natural resources above and below the ground, dividing up the world in this way would be (has been) a bloody business. And once the wars start, the divisions that result are unlikely to be either just or stable.

The problems at the other end of the continuum are of a different kind. Conventional warfare would be impossible in a radically centralized global state, for its agents would have disappeared, and none of the motives for going to war would any longer operate: ethnic and religious differences and divergent national interests, indeed, every kind of sectional interest, would lose their political relevance. Diversity would be radically privatized. In principle, at least, the global state would be constituted solely and entirely by autonomous individuals, free, within the limits of the criminal law, to choose their own life plans.

In practice, however, this constituting principle is radically unlikely to prevail, and ideal types should not be fictional types; they have to fit an imaginable reality. It isn't plausible that the citizens of a global state would be, except for the free choices they make, exactly like one another, all the collective and inherited differences that make for rivalry and distrust today having disappeared in the course of the state's formation. Surely different understandings of how we ought to live would persist; and these would continue to be embodied in ways of life, historical cultures, and religions, commanding strong loyalties and seeking public expression. So let me redescribe the global state. Groups of many different sorts would continue to shape the lives of their members in significant ways, but their existence would be largely ignored by the central authorities; particularistic interests would be overridden; demands for the public expression of cultural divergence would be rejected.

The reason for the rejection is easily explained: the global state would be much like states today, only on a vastly greater scale. If it were to sustain itself over time, it too would have to command the loyalty of its citizens and give expression to a political culture distinctly its own. It would have to look legitimate to everyone in the world. Given this necessity, I don't see how it could accommodate anything like the range of cultural and religious difference that we see around us today. Even a global state committed to toleration would be limited in its powers of accommodation by its prior commitment to what I will call "globalism," that is, centralized rule over the whole world. For some cultures and most orthodox religions can only survive if they are permitted degrees of separation that are incompatible with globalism. And so the survival of these groups would be at risk; under the rules of the global state, they would not be able to sustain and pass on their way of life. This is the meaning I would give to Kant's warning that a cosmopolitan constitution could lead to "terrifying despotism" (*Theory and Practice*, Part III) — the danger is less to individuals than to groups. A more genuine regime of global toleration would have to make room for cultural and religious autonomy, but that would involve a move rightward on the continuum.

Once again, however, I want to acknowledge the advantages that lie on the continuum's far left side, though in this case they are more hypothetical than actual, since we have less experience of centralization than of anarchy. But we can generalize from the history of centralized states and suggest that global distributive justice might be better served by a strong government able to establish universal standards of labor and welfare and to shift resources from richer to poorer countries. Of course, the will to undertake egalitarian reforms might well be absent in the world republic — just as it is in most sovereign states today. But at least the capacity would exist; the European Community (EC) provides some modest but not insignificant examples of the redistribution that centralized power makes possible. At the same time, however, the strength of the single center carries with it the threat of tyranny.

Now let's move one step in from the left side of the continuum, which brings us to a global regime that has the form of a *Pax Romana*. It is centralized through the hegemony of a single great power over all the lesser powers of international society. This hegemony sustains world peace, even if there are intermittent rebellions, and it does this while still permitting some degree of cultural independence — perhaps in a form like that of the Ottoman *millet* system, under which different religious groups were granted partial legal autonomy. The autonomy is not secure, because the center is always capable of canceling it; nor will it necessarily take the form most desired by a particular group. It isn't negotiated between equals but granted by the powerful to the weak. Nonetheless, arrangements of this sort represent the most stable regime of toleration known in world history. The rulers of the empire recognize the value (at least, the prudential value) of group autonomy, and this recognition has worked very effectively for group survival. But the rulers obviously don't recognize individual citizens as participants in the government of the empire, they don't protect individuals against their own groups, and they don't aim at an equitable distribution of resources among either groups or individuals. Imperial hegemony is a form of political inequality that commonly makes for further inequalities in the economy and in social life generally.

I have to be careful in writing about imperial rule, because I am a citizen of the only state in the contemporary world capable of aspiring to it. That's not my own aspiration for my country, nor do I really think that it's possible, but I won't pretend to believe that a *Pax Americana*, however undesirable, is the worst thing that could happen to the world today (it may be the worst thing that could happen to America), and I have been an advocate of a more activist American political/military role in places like Rwanda and Kosovo. But a role of that sort is still far from imperial hegemony, which, though we might value it for the peace it brought (or just for an end to the massacres), is clearly not one of the preferred regimes. It would reduce some of the risks of a global state, but not in a stable way, because imperial power is often arbitrary and capricious. And even if a particular empire did protect communal autonomy, it would be of no use to individuals trapped in oppressive communities.

Now let's move in from the right side of the continuum: one step from anarchy brings us to something like the current arrangement of international society (hence this is the least idealized of my ideal types). We see in the world today a series of global organizations of a political, economic, and judicial sort — the United Nations, the World Bank, the International Monetary Fund (IMF), the World Trade Organization (WTO), the World Court, and so on — that serve to modify state sovereignty. No state possesses the absolute sovereignty described by early modern political theorists, which makes for anarchy in its strongest sense. On the other hand, the global organizations are weak; their decision mechanisms are uncertain and slow; their powers of enforcement are difficult to bring to bear and, at best, only partially effective. Warfare between or among states has been reduced, but overall violence has not been reduced. There are many weak, divided, and unstable states in the world today, and the global regime has not been successful in preventing civil wars, military interventions, savage repression of political enemies, massacres, and "ethnic cleansing" aimed at minority populations. Nor has global inequality been reduced, even though the flow of capital across borders (labor mobility too, I think) is easier than it has ever been — and, according to theorists of the free market, this ought to have egalitarian effects. All in all, we cannot be happy with the current state of the world; indeed, the combination of (many) weak states with weak global organizations brings disadvantages from both directions: the protection of ethnic and religious difference is inadequate and so is the protection of individual rights and the promotion of equality.

So we need to move further toward centralization. The next step doesn't bring us to, say, a United Nations with its own army and police force or a World Bank with a single currency. In terms of intellectual strategy, we would do better to reach arrangements of that kind from the other side. Consider instead the same "constitutional" arrangements that we currently have, reinforced by a much stronger international civil society. Contemporary political theorists argue that civil society has often served to strengthen the democratic state. Certainly, associations that engage, train, and empower ordinary men and women serve democracy more effectively than other regimes, but they probably

strengthen any state that encourages rather than suppresses asso-
ciational life. Would they also strengthen the semi-governmental
international organizations that now exist? I am inclined to think
that they already do this in modest ways and could do so much
more extensively.

Imagine a wide range of civic associations — for mutual aid,
human rights advocacy, the protection of minorities, the achievement of gender equality, the defense of the environment, the
advancement of labor — organized on a much larger scale than at
present. All these groups would have centers distinct from the
centers of particular states; they would operate across state borders and recruit activists and supporters without reference to
nationality. And all of them would be engaged in activities of the
sort that governments also ought to be engaged in — and where
governmental engagement is more effective when it is seconded
(or even initiated) by citizen-volunteers. Once the volunteers
were numerous enough, they would bring pressure to bear on
particular states to cooperate with each other and with global
agencies; and their own work would enhance the effectiveness of
the cooperation.

But these associations of volunteers co-exist in international
civil society with multinational corporations that command armies of well-paid professional and managerial employees and
threaten to overwhelm all other global actors. This is still a
threat, not an achievement — the corporations haven't entirely
escaped the control of the nation-state — but the threat isn't
imaginary. And I can describe only an imaginary set of balancing
forces in an expanded civil society: multinational labor unions,
for example, and political parties operating across national fron-
tiers. Of course, in a global state or a world empire, multinational
corporations would be instantly domesticated, since there would

be no place for their multiplication, no borders for them to cross. But that isn't an automatic solution to the problems they create; in domestic society, exactly as in international society, they challenge the regulative and redistributive power of the political authorities. They require a practical, political response, and international civil society provides the best available space for the development of this politics.

Best available, but not necessarily sufficient for the task: it is a feature of the associations of civil society that they run after problems; they react to crises; their ability to anticipate, plan, and prevent lags far behind that of the state. Their activists are more likely to minister heroically to the victims of a plague than to enforce public health measures in advance. They arrive in the battle zone only in time to assist the wounded and shelter the refugees. They struggle to organize a strike against low wages and brutal working conditions, but are unable to shape the economy. They protest environmental disasters that are already disastrous. Even when they predict coming troubles, they have too little institutional power to act effectively; they are not responsible for the state as a whole, and their warnings are often disregarded precisely because they are seen as irresponsible. As for the underlying, long-term problems of international society — insecurity and inequality above all — civil associations are at best mitigating factors: their activists can do many good things, but they can't make peace in a country torn by civil war or redistribute resources on a significant scale.

I want to take another step in from the left side of the continuum, but will first summarize the steps so far. Because this next one, and the one after that, will bring us to what seem to me the most attractive possibilities, I need to characterize, perhaps try to name, the less attractive ones already canvassed. Note first that the right side of the continuum is a realm of pluralism and the left side a realm of unity. I am not happy with that description of right and left; there have always been pluralist tendencies on the left, and those are the tendencies that I identify with. Still, it is probably true that unity has been the dominant ambition of left-ist parties and movements, so it doesn't make much sense, on this occasion anyway, to fiddle with the rightness and leftness of the continuum.

Starting from the right, then, I have marked off three arrange-ments, moving in the direction of greater centralization but doing this, paradoxically, by adding to the pluralism of agents. First, there is the anarchy of states, where there are no effective agents except the governments that act in the name of state sov-ereignty. Next, we add to these governments a plurality of inter-national political and financial organizations, with a kind of authority that limits but doesn't abolish sovereignty. And after that, we add a plurality of international associations that operate across borders and serve to strengthen the constraints on state action. So we have international anarchy and then two degrees of global pluralism.

On the left, I have so far marked off only two arrangements, moving in the direction of greater division but maintaining the idea of a single center. The first is the global state, the least divided of imaginable regimes, whose members are individual men and women. The second is the global empire, whose mem-bers are the subject nations. The hegemony of the imperial na-tion divides it from the others, without abolishing the others.

The next step in from the left brings with it the end of subjec-tion: the new arrangement is a federation of nation-states, a

United States of the World. The strength of the center, of the federal government, will depend on the rights freely ceded to it by the member states and on the direct or indirect character of its jurisdiction over individual citizens. Defenders of what Americans call "states' rights" will argue for a mediated jurisdiction, with fewer rights ceded to the center. Obviously, the greater the mediating role of the member states, the more this arrangement moves rightward on the continuum; if the mediation disappears entirely, we are back at the left end, in the global state. To find a place for this federal regime, we need to imagine a surrender of sovereignty by the member states and then a constitutionally guaranteed functional division of power, such that the states are left with significant responsibilities and the means to fulfill them — a version, then, of the American system, projected internationally. A greatly strengthened United Nations, incorporating the World Bank and the World Court, might approximate this model, so long as it had the power to coerce member states that refused to abide by its resolutions and verdicts. If the U.N. retained its current structure, with the Security Council as it is now constituted, the global federation would be an oligarchy or perhaps, because the General Assembly represents a kind of democracy, a mixed regime. It isn't easy to imagine any other sort of federation, given the current inequalities of wealth and power among states. The oligarchs won't yield their positions, and any effective federal regime would have to accommodate them (though it might also drain their strength over the long run).

These inequalities are probably harder to deal with than any political differences among the states. Even if all the states were republics, as Kant hoped they would be, the federation would still be wholly or partly oligarchic, so long as the existing distribution of resources was unchanged. And oligarchy here represents division; it drastically qualifies the powers of the center. By contrast, the political character of the member states would tend to become more and more similar; here the move would be toward unity or, at least, uniformity. For all the states would be incorporated into the same constitutional structure, bound, for example, by the same codes of social and political rights and far less able than they are today to ignore those rights. Citizens who think themselves oppressed would appeal to the federal courts and presumably find quick redress. Even if the member states were not democracies to start with, they would become uniformly democratic over time.

As a democrat I ought to find this outcome more attractive than I do; the problem is that it's more likely to be reached by pressure from the center than by democratic activism at (to shift my metaphor) the grassroots. Some combination of the two might work fairly well. But I want to stress that my own preference for democracy doesn't extend to a belief that this preference should be uniformly enforced on every political community. Democracy has to be reached through a political process that, in its nature, can also produce different results. Whenever these results threaten life and liberty, some kind of intervention is necessary, but they don't always do that, and when they don't the different political formations that emerge must be given room to develop (and change). But could a global federation make its peace with political pluralism?

It is far more likely to make its peace with material inequality. A federal regime would probably redistribute resources, but only within limits set by its oligarchs (once again, the European Community provides examples). The greater the power acquired by the central government, the more redistribution there is likely to be. But this kind of power would be dangerous to all the member states, not only to the wealthiest among them. It isn't clear how to strike the balance; presumably that would be one of the central issues in the internal politics of the federation (but there wouldn't be any other politics since, by definition, nothing lies outside the federation).

Constitutional guarantees would serve to protect national and ethnic/religious groups. This seems to be Kant's assumption: "In such a league, every nation, even the smallest, can expect to have security and rights . . ." (*Idea for a Universal History with a Cosmopolitan Intent,* Seventh Thesis). In fact, however, only those groups that achieved sovereignty before the federation was formed would have a sure place within it. So there would have to be some procedure for recognizing and securing the rights of new groups, as well as a code of rights for individuals without regard to their memberships. Conceivably, the federal regime would turn out to be a guardian of both eccentric groups and individuals — as in the United States, for example, where embattled minorities and idiosyncratic citizens commonly appeal to the central government when they are mistreated by local authorities. When such an appeal doesn't work, however, Americans have options that would not be available to the citizens of a global union: they can carry their appeal to the U.N. or the World Court or they can move to another country. There is still something to be said for division and pluralism.

Now let's take another step in from the right side and try to imagine a coherent form of division. I have in mind the familiar anarchy of states mitigated and controlled by a threefold set of non-state agents: organizations like the U.N., the associations of international civil society, and regional unions like the EC. This is the third degree of global pluralism, and in its fully developed (ideal) version, it offers the largest number of opportunities for political action on behalf of peace, justice, cultural difference, and individual rights; and it poses, at the same time, the smallest risk of global tyranny. Of course, opportunities for action are no more than that; they bring no guarantees; and conflicts are sure to arise among men and women pursuing these different values. I imagine this last regime as providing a context for politics in its fullest sense and for the widest engagement of ordinary citizens.

THE CONTINUUM

From the left side: UNITY
Global state/Multinational empire/Federation

$\longrightarrow$

From the right side: DIVISION
3rd degree/2nd degree/1st degree of global pluralism/Anarchy

$\longleftarrow$

Consider again the troubling features of the first five, possibly the first six regimes: in some of them it is the decentered world and the self-centered states inhabiting it (whether the states are strong or weak) that threaten our values; in others it is the tyrannical potential of the newly constituted center that poses the danger. So the problem is to overcome the radical decentralization of sovereign states without creating a single all-powerful central regime. And the solution that I want to defend, the third degree of global pluralism, goes roughly like this: create a set of alternative centers and an increasingly dense web of social ties that cross state boundaries. The solution is to build on the institutional structures that now exist, or are slowly coming into existence, and to strengthen all of them, even if they are competitive with one another.

So the third degree of global pluralism requires a U.N. with a military force of its own capable of humanitarian interventions and a strong version of peacekeeping — but still a force that can only be used with the approval of the Security Council or a very large majority of the General Assembly. Then it requires a World Bank and IMF strong enough to regulate the flow of capital and the forms of international investment and a WTO able to enforce labor and environmental standards as well as trade agreements — all these, however, must be independently governed, not tightly coordinated with the U.N. It requires a World Court with power to make arrests on its own, but needing to seek U.N. support in the face of opposition from any of the (semi-sovereign) states of international society. Add to these organizations a very large number of civic associations operating internationally, including political parties that run candidates in different countries' elections and labor unions that realize their long-standing goal of international solidarity, as well as single-issue movements of a more familiar kind. The larger the membership of these associations and the wider their extension across state boundaries, the more they would knit together the politics of the global society. But they would never constitute a single center; they would always represent multiple sources of political energy; they would always be diversely focused.

Now add a new layer of governmental organization — the regional federation, of which the EC is only one possible model. It is necessary to imagine both tighter and looser structures, distributed across the globe, perhaps even with overlapping memberships: differently constituted federal unions in different parts of the world. This would bring many of the advantages of a global federation but with greatly reduced risks of tyranny from the center. For it is a crucial feature of regionalism that there will be many centers.

To appreciate the beauty of this pluralist arrangement, one must attach a greater value to political possibility, and the activism it breeds, than to the certainty of political success. To my mind, certainty is always a fantasy, but I don't want to deny that something is lost when one gives up the more unitary versions of globalism. What is lost is the hope of creating a more egalitarian world with a stroke of the pen — a single legislative act enforced from a single center. And the hope of achieving perpetual peace, the end of conflict and violence, everywhere and forever. And the hope of a singular citizenship and a singular identity for all human individuals — so that they would be autonomous men and women, and nothing else.

I must hurry to deny what the argument so far may suggest to many readers: I don't mean to sacrifice all these hopes solely for the sake of "communitarianism" — that is, for the sake of cultural and religious difference. That last is an important value, and it is no doubt well served by the third degree of pluralism (indeed, the different levels of government allow new opportunities for self-expression and autonomy to minority groups hitherto subordinated within the nation-state). But difference as a value exists alongside peace, equality, and autonomy; it doesn't supercede them. My argument is that all these are best pursued politically in circumstances where there are many avenues of pursuit, many agents in pursuit. The dream of a single agent — the enlightened despot, the civilizing imperium, the communist vanguard, the global state — is a delusion. We need many agents, many arenas of activity and decision. Political values have to be defended in different places so that failure here can be a spur to action there, and success there a model for imitation here.

But there will be failures as well as successes, and before concluding, I need to worry about three possible failures — so as to stress that all the arrangements, including the one I prefer, have their dangers and disadvantages. The first is the possible failure of peacekeeping, which is also, today, a failure to protect ethnic or religious minorities. Wars between and among states will be rare in a densely webbed international society. But the very success of the politics of difference makes for internal conflicts that sometimes reach to "ethnic cleansing" and even genocidal civil war. The claim of all the strongly centered regimes is that this sort of thing will be stopped, but the possible price of doing this, and of maintaining the capacity to do it, is a tyranny without borders, a more "total" regime than the theory of totalitarianism ever envisaged. The danger of all the decentered and multicentered regimes is that no one will stop the awfulness. The third degree of pluralism maximizes the number of agents who might stop it or at least mitigate its effects: individual states acting unilaterally (like the Vietnamese when they shut down the killing fields of Cambodia), alliances and unions of states (like the North Atlantic Treaty Organization in the Kosovo war), global organizations (like the U.N.), and the volunteers of international civil society (like Doctors Without Borders). But there is no assigned agent, no singular responsibility; everything waits for political debate and decision — and may wait too long.

The second possible failure is in the promotion of equality. Here too, the third degree of pluralism provides many opportunities for egalitarian reform, and there will surely be many experiments in different societies or at different levels of government (like the Israeli kibbutz or the Scandinavian welfare state or the EC's redistributive efforts or the proposed "Tobin tax" on international financial transactions). But the forces that oppose equality will never have to face the massed power of the globally dispossessed, for there won't be one global arena where this power can be massed. Instead, many organizations will seek to mobilize the dispossessed and express their aspirations, sometimes cooperating, sometimes competing with one another.

The third possible failure is in the defense of individual liberty. Once again, the pluralism of states, cultures, and religions — even if full sovereignty no longer exists anywhere — means that individuals in different settings will be differently entitled and protected. We can (and should) defend some minimal understanding of human rights and seek its universal enforcement, but enforcement in the third degree of pluralism would necessarily involve many agents, hence many arguments and decisions, and the results are bound to be uneven.

Can a regime open to such failures possibly be the most just regime? I only want to argue that it is the political arrangement that most facilitates the everyday pursuit of justice under conditions least dangerous to the overall cause of justice. All the other regimes are worse, including the one on the far left of the continuum for which the highest hopes have been held out. For it is a mistake to imagine Reason in power in a global state — as great a mistake (and a mistake of the same kind) as to imagine the future world order as a millennial kingdom where God is the king. The rulers required by regimes of this kind don't exist or, at least, don't manifest themselves politically. By contrast, the move toward pluralism suits people like us, all-too-real and no more than intermittently reasonable, for whom politics is a "natural" activity.

Finally, the move to the third degree of pluralism really is a *move*. We are not there yet; we have "many miles to go before we sleep." The kinds of governmental agencies that are needed in an age of globalization haven't yet been developed; the level of participation in international civil society is much too low; regional federations are still in their beginning stages. Reforms in these institutional areas, however, are rarely sought for their own sake. Few people are sufficiently interested. We will strengthen global pluralism only by using it, by seizing the opportunities it offers. There won't be an advance at any institutional level except in the context of a campaign or, better, a series of campaigns for greater security and greater equality for groups and individuals across the globe.

ACKNOWLEDGMENTS

This book is really the creation of my friend Otto Kalscheuer, who first brought these articles together in a book published in Germany with the title *Erklärte Kriege — Kriegserklarungen* (Hamburg: Sabine Groenewold Verlag, 2003). I have added a couple of pieces and moved one to a new place in the book, but basically I have retained his arrangement. I did not think of bringing these essays together until he showed me how to do it.

"The Triumph of Just War Theory (and the Dangers of Success)" was first given as a lecture at a conference organized by Arien Mack at New School University in April 2002; it was published in *Social Research* in the Winter 2002 issue. "Two Kinds of Military Responsibility" was a lecture at the U.S. Military Academy at West Point in May 1980 and was published in *Parameters* in March 1981. "Emergency Ethics" was the Joseph A. Reich, Sr., Distinguished Lecture at the Air Force Academy in November 1988 and was first published as a pamphlet by the academy. "Terrorism: A Critique of Excuses" appeared in *Problems of International Justice*, edited by Steven Luper-Foy (Boulder: Westview Press, 1988). "The Politics of Rescue" was written for an earlier New School conference organized by Arien Mack and held in November 1994; it was first published in *Dissent* in Winter 1995 and in *Social Research* later that year.

"Justice and Injustice in the Gulf War" is the preface to the second edition of *Just and Unjust Wars* (New York: Basic Books, 1992). A slightly different version, which I have used here, was published in *But Was It Just? Reflections on the Morality of the*

Persian Gulf War, edited by David E. DeCosse (New York: Doubleday, 1992). "Kosovo" was written for the Summer 1999 issue of *Dissent*. "The *Intifada* and the Green Line" appeared in *The New Republic* under the title "The Green Line: After the Uprising, Israel's New Border" in September 1988. "The Four Wars of Israel/Palestine" was published in the Fall 2002 *Dissent*, and "After 9/11: Five Questions About Terrorism," in the Winter 2002 issue. "Inspectors Yes, War No" appeared in *The New Republic* in September 2002. "The Right Way" was first published in *Le Monde* and the *Frankfurter Rundschau* in January 2003; the version I have used here appeared in *The New York Review of Books* in March. "What a Little War Could Do" was an op-ed piece in *The New York Times* in March 2003. "So, Is This a Just War?" was posted on the *Dissent* Web site the same month, the day after the war began. "Just and Unjust Occupations" was written for this book in November 2003 and published in *Dissent* in the Winter 2004 issue.

"Governing the Globe" was the Multatuli lecture at Leuven University in April 1999; this version was published in *Dissent* in Fall 2000.

I am grateful to all the editors and publishers who provided me with the space I needed to make my arguments, especially to my colleagues at *Dissent* magazine and to Marty Peretz and Peter Beinert of *The New Republic*, who published my articles even when they strongly disagreed with them. I owe many people thanks for comments, criticism, and encouragement — among them Joanne Barkan, Gary Bass, Leo Casey, Mitchell Cohen, Michael Doyle, Jean Bethke Elshtain, Clifford Geertz, Todd Gitlin, Anthony Hartle, Stanley Hauerwas, Brian Hehir, Stanley Hoffmann, James Turner Johnson, Michael Kazin, Ted Koontz,

ACKNOWLEDGMENTS

Terry Nardin, Brian Orend, Bart Pattyn, Jim Rule, Henry Shue, Ann Snitow, and Malham M. Wakin. Judy Walzer read most of these pieces, in one version or another, and marked in the margins the sentences that I would regret (and then I rewrote them). Ame Dyckman kept track of all the different versions of these articles and collected the necessary permissions to reprint them.

I want to take this occasion to remember Martin Kessler, the editor at Basic Books who worked with me on *Just and Unjust Wars*, who is largely responsible for getting me into this business. I suppose that I had gotten myself into it as a citizen and political activist, but it was Martin who first suggested that I write a book and then looked over my shoulder during the years of writing.

NOTES

Chapter 1. The Triumph of Just War Theory
(and the Dangers of Success)

1. Augustine's argument on just war can be found in *The Political Writings of St. Augustine*, ed. Henry Paolucci (Chicago: Henry Regnery, 1962), 162–83; modern readers will need a commentary: see Herbert A. Dean, *The Political and Social Ideas of St. Augustine* (New York: Columbia University Press, 1963), 134–71.

2. See Francisco deVitoria, *Political Writings*, ed. Anthony Pagden and Jeremy Lawrance (Cambridge: Cambridge University Press, 1991), 302–4, and for commentary, see James Turner Johnson, *Ideology, Reason, and the Limitation of War: Religious and Secular Concepts, 1200–1740* (Princeton: Princeton University Press, 1975), 150–71.

3. See James Boswell, *Life of Samuel Johnson LL.D.*, ed. Robert Maynard Hutchins, vol. 44 of *Great Books of the Western World* (Chicago: Encyclopedia Britannica, 1952), 129, quoting Dr. Johnson: " 'I love the University of Salamanca, for when the Spaniards were in doubt as to the lawfulness of conquering America, the University of Salamanca gave it as their opinion that it was not lawful.' He spoke this with great emotion."

4. With some hesitation, I cite my own discussion of military necessity (and the references there to more sympathetic treatments): Michael Walzer, *Just and Unjust Wars* (New York: Basic Books, 1977), 144–51, 239–42, 251–55.

5. The best discussion of the realists is Michael Joseph Smith, *Realist Thought from Weber to Kissinger* (Baton Rouge: Louisiana State University Press, 1986); chapter 6, on Hans Morgenthau, is especially relevant to my argument here.

6. Anthony Hartle is one of those veterans, who eventually wrote his own book on the ethics of war: Anthony E. Hartle, *Moral Issues in Military Decision Making* (Lawrence: University Press of Kansas, 1989).

7. See the documents collected in *The Gulf War: History, Documents, Opinions*, ed. Micah L. Sifry and Christopher Cerf (New York: Times Books, 1991), 197–352, among them Bush's speeches and a wide range of other opinion papers.

8. I made the case against attacks on infrastructural targets immediately after the war (but others made it earlier) in *But Was It Just? Reflections on the Morality of the Persian Gulf War*, ed. David E. DeCosse (New York: Doubleday, 1992), 12–13.

9. Stanley Fish's op-ed piece in *The New York Times* (October 15, 2001) provides an example of the postmodernist argument in its most intelligent version.

10. This argument was made by several participants at a conference on humanitarian intervention held at the Zentrum für interdisziplinare Forschung, Bielefeld University, Germany, in January 2002.

11. "A life is paid for by another life, and from these two sacrifices springs the promise of a value." Albert Camus, *The Rebel*, trans. Anthony Bower (New York: Vintage, 1956), 169. See also the argument in act I of *The Just Assassins*, in Albert Camus, *Caligula and Three Other Plays*, trans. Stuart Gilbert (New York: Vintage, 1958), esp. 246–47.

12. For arguments in favor of using ground forces in Kosovo, see William Joseph Buckley, ed., *Kosovo: Contending Voices on Balkan Interventions* (Grand Rapids, Mich.: William B. Eerdmans, 2000), 293–94, 333–35, 342.

13. Bush's statement on stopping the American advance, and his declaration of victory, can be found in *The Gulf War: History, Documents, Opinions*, 449–51; arguments for and against stopping can be found in *But Was It Just?* 13–14, 29–32.

14. Artyom Borovik's *The Hidden War: A Russian Journalist's Account of the Soviet War in Afghanistan* (London: Faber and Faber, 1990) provides a useful, though highly personal, account of the Russian war in Afghanistan; for an academic history, see Larry P. Goodson, *Afghanistan's Endless War: State Failure, Regional Politics, and the Rise of the Taliban* (Seattle: University of Washington Press, 2001).

Chapter 3. Emergency Ethics

1. Winston Churchill, *The Gathering Storm* (New York: Bantam Books, 1961), 488.

2. Michael Walzer, *Just and Unjust Wars* (New York: Basic Books, 1977), chapter 16.

3. Churchill himself was entirely straightforward; see *The Hinge of Fate* (New York: Bantam Books, 1962), 770: the aim of the bombing was "to create conditions intolerable to the mass of the German population." This is from a memorandum written in July 1942.

4. For an effort to escape the contradictions (using examples from domestic society rather than from war), see Alan Donagan, *The Theory of Morality* (Chicago: University of Chicago Press, 1977), 184–89.

5. These two positions are put forward in near classic form in Thomas Nagel, "War and Massacre," and R. B. Brandt, "Utilitarianism and the Rules of War," which appeared together in *Philosophy and Public Affairs* 1, no. 2 (winter 1972): 123–65.

6. See, for example, Ronald Dworkin, *Taking Rights Seriously* (Cambridge, Mass.: Harvard University Press, 1977).

7. Niccolò Machiavelli, *The Prince and the Discourses*, intro. by Max Lerner (New York: The Modern Library, 1950), 139.

8. But see Telford Taylor, *Nuremberg and Vietnam: An American Tragedy* (Chicago: Quadrangle Books, 1970), 36.

9. In a critical review of *Just and Unjust Wars*, Kenneth Brown writes that "throughout his work, Walzer identifies the highest human aspirations with the supremacy of the nation-state" (Brown, " 'Supreme Emergency': A Critique of Michael Walzer's Moral Justification for Allied Obliteration Bombing in World War II," *Journal of World Peace* 1, no. 1 [spring 1984]). No, I make no argument for the "supremacy" of the nation-state, only for its existence, and only insofar as its existence serves the communal purposes I describe in this essay.

10. Edmund Burke, *Reflections on the Revolution in France* (London: J. M. Dent, 1910), 93.

11. On the neutral state, see Ronald Dworkin, "Liberalism," in *Pub-*

lic and Private Morality, ed. Stuart Hampshire (Cambridge: Cambridge University Press, 1978).

12. See Hobbes's discussion of military service in *Leviathan*, part 2, chapter 21, and my own commentary, "The Obligation to Die for the State," in *Obligations* (Cambridge, Mass.: Harvard University Press, 1970).

13. Camus, *The Just Assassins*, in *Caligula and Three Other Plays*, trans. Stuart Gilbert (New York: Vintage, 1958).

14. See my "Political Action: The Problem of Dirty Hands," *Philosophy and Public Affairs* 2, no. 2 (winter 1973): 160–80.

Chapter 4. Terrorism: A Critique of Excuses

1. I cannot resist a few examples: Edward Said, "The Terrorism Scam," *The Nation*, June 14, 1986; and (more intelligent and circumspect) Richard Falk, "Thinking About Terrorism," *The Nation*, June 28, 1986.

2. Machiavelli, *The Discourses* I:ix. As yet, however, there have been no results that would constitute a Machiavellian excuse.

3. See, for example, Daniel Goleman, "The Roots of Terrorism Are Found in Brutality of Shattered Childhood," *New York Times*, September 2, 1986, pp. C1, 8. Goleman discusses the psychological and social history of particular terrorists, not the roots of terrorism.

4. The neoconservative position is represented, although not as explicitly as I have stated it here, in Benjamin Netanyahu, ed., *Terrorism: How the West Can Win* (New York: Farrar, Straus & Giroux, 1986).

5. The reason the terrorist strategy, however indecent in itself, cannot be instrumental to some decent political purpose is because any decent purpose must somehow accommodate the people against whom the terrorism is aimed, and what terrorism expresses is precisely the refusal of such an accommodation, the radical devaluing of the Other. See my argument in *Just and Unjust Wars* (New York: Basic Books, 1977), 197–206, especially 203.

6. Aristotle, *The Politics* 1313–1314a.

CREDITS

Grateful acknowledgment is made for permission to reprint the following articles, essays, and lectures:

"After 9/11: Five Questions About Terrorism," *Dissent* (Winter 2002): 5–16; "The Four Wars of Israel/Palestine," *Dissent* (Fall 2002): 26–33; "Governing the Globe," *Dissent* (Fall 2000): 44–51; "Kosovo," *Dissent* (Summer 1999): 5–7; "The Politics of Rescue," *Dissent* (Winter 1995): 35–41; "So, Is This a Just War?" *Dissent* (Web exclusive, posted March 20, 2003). All six pieces are reprinted with permission of *Dissent*.

"Emergency Ethics," *The Joseph A. Reich, Sr., Distinguished Lecture on War, Morality, and the Military Profession*, no. 1 (November 21, 1988). Delivered at the U.S. Air Force Academy, Colo. Reprinted with permission of the Academy.

"The Green Line: After the Uprising, Israel's New Border," *The New Republic* 199 (September 5, 1988): 22–24; "No Strikes: Inspectors Yes, War No," *The New Republic* 227 (September 30, 2002): 19–22. Both pieces are reprinted with permission of *The New Republic*.

"Justice and Injustice in the Gulf War" was originally "Preface to the Second Edition: After the Gulf," in Michael Walzer, *Just and Unjust Wars: A Moral Argument with Historical Illustrations* (New York: Basic Books, 1992): xi–xxiii. "Terrorism: A Critique of Excuses," appeared in Steven Luper-Foy, ed., *Problems of International Justice* (Boulder, Colo.: Westview Press, 1988): 237–247. Basic Books and Westview Press are members of the Perseus Books Group, New York, N.Y. Both pieces are reprinted with permission from Perseus Books Group.

"The Right Way," *The New York Review of Books* L4 (March 13, 2003): 4. Reprinted with permission from *The New York Review of Books* © 2003 NYREV, Inc.

"The Triumph of Just War Theory (and the Dangers of Success)," © *Social Research* 69, no. 4 (Winter 2002): 925–944. Reprinted with permission.

INDEX